MARIE HOLM

Quivering Desserts

&

other puddings

GRUB STREET • LONDON

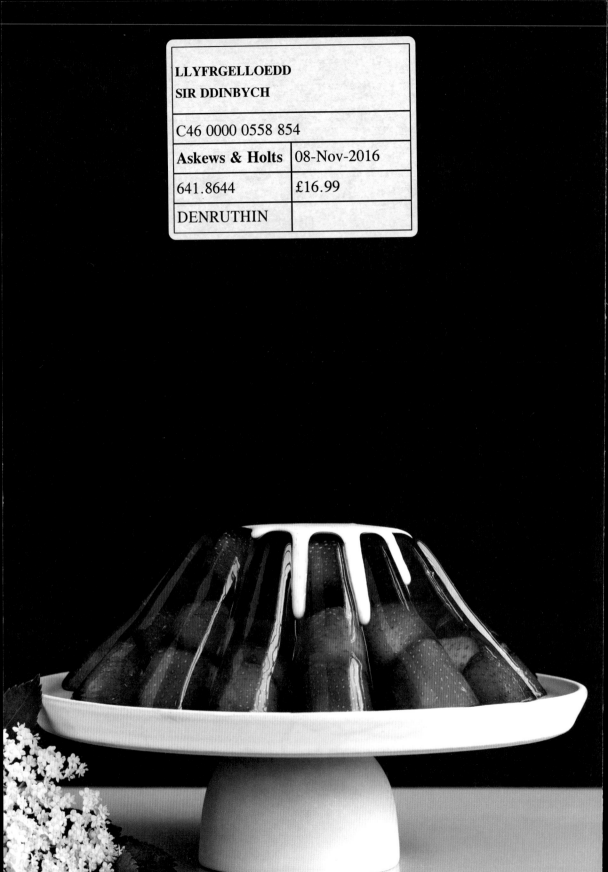

CONTENTS

BRING BACK PUDDINGS!

What I refer to as pudding – the ones that I make and love, the ones that are featured in this book – are custard-based, wobbly desserts that go by the name of crème bavaroise in French cuisine. This is also known as Bavarian cream or simply bavarois in English. Bavarois puddings basically consist of a crème anglaise – a custard containing milk, cream, sugar and egg yolks – flavoured with fruit, spices, liqueurs or spirits, chocolate, juice, tea or flowers, then set with gelatine and given lightness with a good helping of whipped cream. So I have decided to keep the name 'pudding' for most of the recipes in the book; however, I have used the word bavarois to refer to the classic vanilla version on page 40.

The first time I tasted a home-made bavarois pudding, was at a museum – of all places. In 2009, I visited an open air museum, and there in the kitchen of a small manor house, stood a cook in a starched apron, cooking puddings in the same way as they had been made in rural households in the early 1900s. I was sold from the very first gelatinous bite!

I had eaten more than enough pudding as a child, but at the time it was the Dr. Oetker yellow powdered variety, which I still ate with great pleasure. I also had a childish soft spot for the plastic-looking puddings from the German supermarkets where we would get our food when my family drove south during the summer holidays.

So, in one way or another, I was destined as an adult to fall wildly and passionately in love – first with pudding, and then with the idea of bringing back this wonderful old-fashioned dessert.

But back to that first pudding. When I got home, I knew right away that I had to recreate the art of that cook. And so I started to search for puddings in old books and magazines, and to create my own recipes. Nostalgia and early memories of food are perhaps the most important factors when it comes to taste preferences, so my first attempt at the art of pudding making was to recreate the pudding of my childhood. I gave it a Dr. Oetker-like texture and the very special taste of mock almond.

It was a success. I made the pudding in my summer house, which being a 1962 shoebox was the perfect setting for my reacquantaince with this old-school dessert. It made sense to eat the yellow pudding out of a 1960s Polish glazed earthenware dish decorated with large flowers, and to offer the dish around to my family who were perched on FDB chairs in the small, dark, wooden house, while a scantily-clad pin-up girl looked down at us from a Christel drawing on the wall.

I had made blackberry sauce for my pudding masterpiece, and the reaction to it was hilarious. The wobbling pudding made us giggle and throw meaning-ful glances at each other across the table. Nobody can gaze at a pudding in motion without thinking that there's something slightly naughty about it! I think that was when I noticed.

In the kitchen at the open air museum, the puddings had almost resembled statues. The stiffened expression of a bygone era, those graceful sculptures stood so still, as did time at the museum. In my summer cottage the pudding wobbled and swayed merrily, and was brought to life by those who shared in its eating, by hands that couldn't help but shake the dish as it was passed around.

But as this was happening in the physical space, ironically, we felt distanced from our saucy 'retro dessert'. Had I been on Instagram at the time, that would probably have been just the hashtag I would have used! "Eating pudding in a shoebox, #eatme #jigglewiggle #housewifeporn #retrodessert." The pudding was fantastic in many ways. It tasted of heavy vanilla pastry cream, and when you put a spoonful into your mouth and pressed your tongue against your palate, it gave it just the right childish squidge – the kind that also works so well with lemon mousse. But it was also something of a prop in my private 60s theatre, an object that looked good in my kitsch holiday home among my flea-market finds.

Back home in my apartment in Co-penhagen, I wrote the recipe down; it had been an almond pudding with amaretto. I made it again for a girlfriend's birthday and topped it with maraschino cherries – which did not make it any more respectable – and we had a good laugh! The Polish earthenware dish was replaced by a streamlined, black and white Design Letters dish, which did help a little, if only from a distance. What I loved about pudding from the beginning was the ridiculous way in which irony lay just below the surface like a barrier to stop me from surrendering to it completely.

But I finally gave in. When I was writing a book of essays on food shortly afterwards, I knew that I had to have a chapter on pudding.

And I began to wonder: why had pudding been consigned to oblivion, and to such an extent that I had to go to a museum to experience it? And why has there not been a pudding revival, when so many other old-fashioned desserts have been brought back to life? And yet others are still with us.

Lemon mousse and ymer (fermented milk) mousse are now all the rage in restaurants and in private homes – the former had never left the limelight. In my essay on puddings I pondered: "Is pudding, with its wobbly, iconic shape, simply bad taste? Is it too artificial? Is it dessert's answer to silicone breast implants?"

My theory was, and still is, that the Dr. Oetker powdered mix has given pudding a reputation of artificiality which, combined with our present-day veneration of the simple, pure and natural, has banished pudding from our tables. When we eat out or come across desserts in social media, we see a stylish, pared-back presentation and organically shaped creations, decorated with wild herbs and flowers. What's so cool about an opulent and artfully shaped pudding topped with a luminescent maraschino cherry?

A few months later, when I stood with four beautiful puddings on display at a stand in a department store, a nice man came up to me and asked without reservations: "Are they real?" Right then and there was the answer to the questions I had asked in my essay. Puddings LOOK artificial (the poor man didn't know anything about my ironic comparison with breast implants and must have been wondering why I was suppressing a snigger while I assured him that everything was completely real!).

The experience did more than just make me smile. It got me thinking that pudding has to distance itself from its artificial, kitsch, pin-up image. And also from the image of being dusty, stuffy and consigned to a museum. For although puddings do have this reputation, they are so much more. A pudding is also genuine, natural, authentic, living, nostalgic, classic – and therefore, of our time, contemporary.

A home-made pudding is a combination of simple, good ingredients that come together with short cooking time and a few hours of impatient waiting while it sets in the refrigerator. Pudding is our cultural history and – depending on our age – our mother, grandmother or great-grandmother's artistry and forgotten kitchen skills all rolled into one wobbly dessert. And therefore pudding has the potential to become modern again, like the other old-fashioned desserts that have gone before, as soon as we decide to give it a new image – one which is deserved and not just the result of a Dr. Oetker packet.

It's ridiculous that a dessert lover like me should have to go to a museum to taste a home-made pudding. But, unfortunately, that's the way things are. Not long ago I was asked to give a masterclass on chocolate pudding in connection with a chocolate company's annual chocolate festival. I took advantage of the opportunity to ask whether there was anybody in the audience who had ever tasted pudding. Most of the 50 or

so people in attendance said that they had. But when I followed up my first question by asking how many of them had tasted a home-made pudding, only one person raised her hand.

Shortly after, I began the process of developing recipes for the book you are now reading, and in that process I set myself the goal of bringing pudding back into fashion. Because the more I learned about pudding, the more I found it sad that others did not have the opportunity to experience just how great a dessert it really is. Like when you fall in love and just want to shout from the rooftops: HERE IS SOMETHING WONDERFUL AND I WANT EVERYONE TO SEE IT!

So, dear reader, you and I have a task before us. Let's join forces to start a wobbly revolution and bring back puddings! And let's start here, in the best possible place: at home in our own kitchens.

Happy reading, and long live the pudding!

Marie

WHY PUDDINGS WENT OUT OF FASHION

Bavarian cream pudding or bavarois was first mentioned in texts dating from the early 1800s, created by the founder of French haute cuisine, Antonin Carême. This extravagant moulded dessert became the height of fashion during the latter half of the 19th century.

These puddings were packed with precious ingredients such as vanilla, rum and dried fruits – and cream, which was hard to get hold of in cities. With the growth of the dairy industry and cooperatives in the late 19th century, whipping cream became increasingly accessible and pudding became a dessert for the general population.

By the end of the 1890s Dr. Oetker had begun to produce powdered pudding mix in Germany, but those packets featuring the profile of a blonde against a red background only became fashionable for the masses after the Second World War. Until then, housewives and cooks would make their puddings using eggs, sugar, milk and cream. And quite a few of them, especially housewives, made stodgier, less expensive, 'porridge puddings', made using barley, cornflour or manna groats, and consisting mainly of cooked, sweetened milk porridge with added egg yolks and sugar, aerated with beaten egg whites and set in a pudding mould, either with gelatine or by cooking in a bain-marie. These were cheap desserts, and cream was only required as an accompaniment, not as an essential ingredient.

Likewise, Dr. Oetker strongly emphasised the affordability of their puddings in post-war advertisements, which may well have been instrumental in the eventual triumph of powdered pudding over the real thing. I own a small original Dr. Oetker recipe booklet from around 1950 and in it you can read the following:

"One of the key questions housewives ask is: What can be done with only a little money to put food on the table that is still nutritious, easily digested and tasty? There is an easy solution, and no magic is required. All of these demands can be fully satisfied with half a litre of milk, some sugar and one packet of Dr. Oetker brand vanilla, almond or chocolate pudding mix. In particular, it contains nutrient salts which are of the greatest importance, as they are equally valuable for children and adults. For all of those who cannot tolerate or who dislike milk, enjoyment of a pudding is of great value, as they receive this important nutrient in a pleasant way. Science teaches us the importance of a varied diet. Pudding brings both pleasant and necessary variety to the daily diet. The fine aroma and highly delicious flavour of pudding act kindly on the digestion and result in even less plentiful meals being absorbed and utilized better, whenever such are served. ... Dr. Oetker puddings are recommended as a complete supper for children as these puddings facilitate digestion, encouraging restful sleep."

There is almost no limit to all the goodness in pudding; and while it is obviously amusing to read today, such claims would make Dr. Oetker front page news! But in the 1950s and afterwards, it was considered cheap and good – any cheap, artificial rubbish was considered better than the real thing – and powdered pudding with canned pineapple beat a classic, home-made vanilla bavarois with red juice sauce any time. Pudding made with the powdered mix became so popular that by the time of my childhood in the 1980s, we had forgotten all about the home-made version. The Dairy Association did include a pudding recipe in one of their recipe booklets, and there would have been the odd pudding lover who continued to hold out. But the fact is that the home-made pudding disappeared from our collective consciousness, from our dessert cookbooks and our kitchens some time after 1945 and before 1980.

PUDDING
the comeback

There are so many good reasons to bring pudding back to the table. Besides the obvious ones – its lovely taste, our common food history, the preservation of good craftsmanship – there are many other significant reasons why pudding deserves a place in the modern kitchen...

1. **PUDDING NEEDS TO BE PREPARED IN ADVANCE.**

   This is a smart move, both when you have guests, and therefore you are sure to have plenty of other things to prepare on the day, and for long, busy weekdays, when you want a dessert that can be there waiting for you in the fridge when you get home. A pudding in its mould can easily keep for as long as 4–5 days in the refrigerator.

2. **PUDDINGS OFFER ENDLESS VARIATIONS.**

   Once you understand the basic principles of making a custard and flavouring it, there is no end to what you can add to it. If you follow my lemon pudding recipe, you can simply switch the lemon juice for grape, bergamot orange or lime juice – there you have a new variation. Puddings with liqueur can also be easily adapted. Use the recipe for rum pudding and swap the rum for calvados or whisky – or try replacing the amaretto in the almond pudding with another liqueur. Puddings with fruit and berries can easily be varied by using other types of purées with roughly the same texture and sweetness, and you can, of course, easily adjust the sweetness by using more or less sugar. You just need to make sure not to use fresh pineapple or kiwi fruit, both of which contain enzymes that are incompatible with gelatine. Puddings in which the cream mixture for the custard base is infused with vanilla, lemon peel, tea or geranium can easily be transformed by replacing these with other spices and flavours. And all of the jellies, both the stand-alone ones and the ones that are used as a shiny topping for a pudding, can be made with other juices or sweetened wine and matching fruit fillings.

3. **PUDDING LOOKS AMAZING WITH LITTLE EFFORT.**

Once you've poured the cream into the mould, the decorative work is actually done! Just unmould it and maybe add a handful of berries or a flower on top, and there you have a beautiful dessert that will impress even the makers of the wildest cakes and desserts.

4. **PUDDING CAN BE SUBSTITUTED FOR A LAYER CAKE ON FESTIVE OCCASIONS.**

Its ability to impress, day-before preparation and infinite variations make a pudding a great centrepiece for birthdays, afternoon get-togethers, student dinners or even weddings.

A pudding can be moulded into a shape that suits the occasion, and it can be decorated with flags, carnations, baby's breath or a plastic bride and groom, depending on the celebration to which it will bring a sweet ending.

5. **PUDDING LOOKS GREAT ON INSTAGRAM!**

Okay, I realize that this may not be the most convincing argument in favour of pudding, but if you like posting food pictures on Instagram, Facebook or other image-based social media, a pudding is sure to score a lot of likes! They are simply incredibly photogenic. And if you're thinking of posting a pudding picture, I personally hope that you will hashtag it with #bringbackpudding or #quiveringdesserts, so that I too can have the opportunity to marvel at your work of pudding art...

THE DIFFERENCE BETWEEN
a bavarois & a mousse

Bavarois and mousse share most of their ingredients, and they mainly consists of cream, sugar and beaten eggs. Bavarois also contains milk, whereas mousse does not, and the latter sometimes contains egg whites instead of cream.

The big difference is in the use of heat. While a custard-based pudding is heated at some point during the preparation – either at the custard stage or in the mould (like the classic crème caramel), a mousse is never cooked. This gives both a different taste and consistency. There is also a difference in the amount of air they contain. Mousse contains almost pure air trapped in the whipped egg whites or whipped cream, while the cream content of a bavarois gives it a much denser consistency – and, of course, its delightful wobble.

Historically, bavarois is the forerunner of a mousse. Bavarois came first, and mousse arrived once whipping cream became more accessible, as a kind of pudding made from cold ingredients, and made much lighter with the fancy whipped cream. And then there is one more thing that distinguishes the two: the way they are shaped. A bavarois is set in a mould, while mousse congeals in a bowl.

HOW TO MAKE A BAVAROIS

The starting point for bavarois, and most of this book's pudding recipes, is crème anglaise. Crème anglaise is a custard. It is made by adding warm, vanilla-scented sweetened milk and cream to lightly beaten egg yolks and sugar, and heating everything up to between 83 and 85°C (180–185°F), so that the mixture thickens.

It is not difficult to make this custard – but there is one thing that can go wrong: if the cream mixture is too hot, it makes the egg yolks coagulate and separate from the liquid, filling the custard with little flecks of scrambled eggs. To prevent this from happening, keep a watchful eye on the cream while it's on the heat...

You will find the recipe for the classic bavarois in each of the recipes in the book, but here is a step-by-step guide to help you through the process.

1. Take out all the necessary ingredients above and weigh them out. Prepare your utensils – you will need a measuring cup, a bowl of water, a heavy-based saucepan, a whisk, a silicone spatula or a wooden spoon, a sieve and two mixing bowls.

2. If using gelatine, start by soaking the leaves in a bowl of cold water. If using vanilla pods, slice them open at this point, scrape out the seeds and mash them together with a little of the previously weighed out sugar to separate the seeds.

3. Combine the milk, cream and vanilla pods together with the vanilla seed and sugar mixture in a heavy-based saucepan. Add a couple of table-spoons of the weighed-out sugar (sugar prevents the cream from burning easily during cooking). Place over a low heat until the milk and cream mixture bubbles along the edge of the pan and is just short of reaching its boiling point. Remove the pan from the heat, cover it with a lid, and allow the vanilla to infuse in the milk and cream mixture for 10–15 minutes.

4. Beat the egg yolks and remaining sugar together lightly in a large bowl just 1–2 minutes by hand with a whisk. The egg and sugar mixture can easily be set aside on the kitchen table without separating while the milk and cream mixture infuses. In fact, this will produce a more stable custard than if you whisk the eggs and sugar together just before add-ing the hot milk and cream mixture.

5. Heat the vanilla-flavoured milk and cream mixture until just short of boiling. Pour it hot into the egg and sugar mixture while whisking vigorously to blend well.

6. Transfer everything back into the pan and heat gently over a low heat while stirring with a silicone spatula if you have one, or use a wooden spoon. The mixture starts off runny, as seen in the photo.

7. TAKE SPECIAL CARE: The custard must NOT boil; it should be heated to approx. 83–85°C (180–185°F), at which point the yolks bind together and the custard thickens. Keep an eye out for the point at which the custard begins to coat the back of the spatula instead of running straight off it. Once it reaches this stage, stop cooking and remove the pan from the heat.

8. It is now time to add the gelatine to the custard, which must be done quickly once you have taken the pan off the heat – the cold gelatine helps to lower the temperature of the custard, whereas the warm custard helps to dissolve the gelatine. Squeeze the excess liquid out of the gelatine and stir it into the custard until it quickly dissolves.

9. Immediately pass the mixture through a sieve into a bowl so that it is not heated any further by the pan. Stir a little to cool if necessary. If you are going to add any flavourings to the custard, such as lemon juice, liqueur or spirit, or fruit purée, now is the time to do it.

10. Cover the custard with cling film in direct contact with its surface to prevent a skin from forming, and leave it in the refrigerator for 1–2 hours where it will chill and possibly set slightly around the edge of the bowl. At this point the custard is ready for the addition of the lightly whipped cream or just for stirring to distribute the vanilla seeds, depending on what kind of pudding you are making. Now for the easy part: pour the bavarois into a suitable mould, place it in the refrigerator and wait for the miracle of setting to happen.

11. N.B. If during step 7 your custard gets too hot and begins to separate or curdle a bit, immediately remove the pan from the heat, pour the mixture into a cold bowl and blend for 30 seconds with a hand-held blender. Pass the custard through a sieve into a clean bowl – hopefully you will have saved it!

GELATINOPHOBIA

I often come across people who are terrified to work with gelatine. They are food lovers who do like airy or wobbly desserts, but who don't dare attempt to make them out of sheer gelatinophobia! "It's separated." "It won't dissolve properly." "There are lumps in it." I can assure you that it is virtually impossible for these fears to be realised when making pudding. If ever gelatine separated or formed lumps in a mousse, it's because it underwent thermal shock when it melted; its state when hot was reversed when added to a cold custard and, so to speak, it was scared stiff!

The advantage of pudding is that the gelatine is not exposed to that kind of shock, because it is added to a warm custard. So fear not. You just need to make sure to soak the leaves of gelatine properly before putting them in the warm custard so that they dissolve and are incorporated evenly into the mixture. And "properly" in practical terms means that you need to make sure to have a large bowl full of cold water and to immerse the gelatine in the water leaf by leaf. This way they won't stick together too much during soaking. Let the gelatine soak for at least 10 minutes or preferably longer before use.

GELATINE
or AGAR-AGAR?

There is a reason for using gelatine in puddings – namely, it's the right gelling agent to produce the exact amount of wobbliness. That being said, you DON'T HAVE TO use animal gelatine. If you are vegetarian or don't eat pork, then fortunately there are alternatives.

I have successfully used isinglass (gelatine made from fish) in many of my puddings. The isinglass I have found comes as a powder, so you have to do a little conversion work. On the other hand, it sets in exactly the same way and with the same strength as the plain leaf gelatine you can find in a supermarket. (1 leaf gelatine weighs 1.7 g, so if the recipe requires 10 leaves, replace with 17 g isinglass powder).

And then there's the plant-based gelling agent agar-agar, which is derived from seaweed and is available in powdered form in health food shops. Agar-agar, on the other hand, sets in a different and more solid way than gelatine, which will take some of the wobble out of your wobbly desserts.

The biggest challenge is that agar-agar melts at a much higher temperature than gelatine; in fact, it has to be boiled in order to work. And most of the puddings in this book are based on custards that must not be allowed to boil! The trick is to boil the agar-agar in some liquid such as lemon juice, fruit juice or amaretto for 2–4 minutes until the mixture is thick and smooth while you make the custard in another saucepan. Add a little of the warm custard to the hot (but not boiling) agar-agar mixture first, and then whisk the agar-agar into the rest of the custard. This works for recipes where there is some kind of liquid that you can use to boil the agar-agar. I can recommend buttermilk pudding, violet/elderflower pudding and lemon pudding, which can be made in this way. Alternatively, you can take part of the total amount of milk required for the custard and use it to boil the agar-agar.

Also note that while gelatine needs to be chilled in order to set, agar-agar sets at room temperature. So if you are making a bavarois with agar-agar, don't wait too long to fold the whipped cream into the custard, and remember that you will have to pour the warm bavarois straight into the mould instead of letting it cool off first. Last but not least, a pudding set with agar-agar is a bit harder to unmould than a pudding set with gelatine. You have to be patient and give it an extra long dip in the hot water before you turn it out (see page 35).

How much agar-agar should you use to set a pudding? As a general rule, use 4 level teaspoons of agar-agar for 1 litre/4 cups of bavarois and make sure that there is at least 150 ml ($^2/_3$ cup) of liquid or more to boil it in. Add a little water if necessary.

A NOTE ABOUT MOULDS

Over the years I have built up a very fine collection of pudding moulds, a collection that is still growing. My first pudding mould is still my favourite, although it isn't technically a pudding mould but an ice-cream mould. I found it in a second-hand shop, where it cost me a paltry few pounds, and it has just the right, deeply fluted shape and a convenient lid. It's aluminium, and it's quite old. Unfortunately, I put it in the dishwasher one day, so now it's no longer quite as pretty. The surface may be a little dull and lacklustre, but it still moulds perfectly well!

The perfect mould gives the pudding a beautiful shape and a fine surface pattern, and it is also designed to make unmoulding easy. Many older moulds have a lid and some of them have a 'chimney' in the middle, originally created to let out steam while the pudding was left to set in a water bath.

If you are looking for a pudding mould, it pays to look at flea markets, second-hand shops and on eBay, where you may be lucky to find fine old specimens in aluminium, copper or tin, or maybe pottery, glass or earthenware. Some of them are hugely expensive (and some of them may have become completely unsuitable for use with food because of their old metal alloys!). I've seen Victorian English copper moulds with towers and ornaments sell for several hundred pounds, Antique ceramic moulds from 1850–1890 sell for about 100 pounds. The latter, however, are both beautiful and useful.

Moulds will be much cheaper if bought new. Many cookware retailers have some lovely ones which can be bought over the internet. They are made of metal with a non-stick coating, and have lids so that they can be used in a water bath and easily be stored in the refrigerator. They are available in two sizes (1 or 2 litres), which cost 20 and 25 pounds, or thereabouts. If you look to countries with a tradition of jelly making, you can find jelly moulds in hard plastic and with smart features housewives will love, such as an aeration lid at the bottom. Check out Amazon.co.uk or Etsy.com where there is a decent selection.

However, perhaps you have an acute craving for pudding which can't be put off until you've bought the right mould, or maybe this is not the kind of thing that you are able to spend a lot of money on. Rest assured; there are other options! I have moulded puddings in plastic tubs, small mixing bowls, cake tins (brioche or kugelhopf tins are perfect) and enamel ring moulds, and I've managed to make very fine round, oblong and square puddings in them. They can easily be turned out as long as you make sure to set them in a rigid container with a smooth surface, and once they are bedecked with whipped cream, berries and flowers, Tupperware won't be the first word that springs to mind!

Finally, you can always forget about all of that and simply pour your bavarois into a nice serving bowl, and then you can dish it out with a spoon, like with mousse. But you and your companions, if that's the case, will be missing out on the most characteristic and wonderful thing about pudding: its wobbliness. A beautiful, moulded and wobbly pudding brought to the table can make even the most obstinate dessert deniers gasp with delight. I usually say that a real pudding should sway as softly as the backside of a peasant girl. If you've ever laid eyes on such a thing, then you know exactly what I mean... If not, I'm sure you can imagine how mesmerising it must be.

How big
SHOULD THE MOULD BE?

In order to find a suitable mould for your pudding, you of course need to know the amount of bavarois you are making, which you can find out from the recipe, and how much of it your mould can hold.

The first part is easy – the amount is indicated in all of the recipes. The second part is actually just as easy. Simply fill your chosen mould up with water, and then pour the water straight into a measuring jug so that you can see if the mould holds 1 litre/4 cups, 1.5 litres, 1.7 litres, or any other volume. And then choose a mould that fits the requirements for your pudding.

If you end up with extra bavarois after filling the mould, it can be set in small bowls or cups, which are lovely to find in the fridge a few days later. Small bowls and smaller moulds are also useful if you are short of time. By dividing the bavarois up into several smaller portions, you reduce the setting time and you won't have to wait nearly as long to be able to serve your pudding.

DECORATING WITH FLOWERS
(and thinking about it)

Fresh flowers make a simple and beautiful decoration for puddings and jellies. They can be placed either around the edge of the pudding or planted right in the middle of it as a final flourish for your wobbly custard masterpiece. Edible flowers such as violets, lilacs, marigolds, roses, elderflowers, nasturtium, borage flowers and pansies are very suitable.

I have a weakness for peonies, although they are actually quite toxic; but when they're in full bloom, their pompom heads simply cry out to crown a pudding. Since peonies are not edible, I use them to decorate puddings that have been set in moulds with a chimney. They have a well in the middle that is perfect for holding a flower stem and act as a vase for the flower. When I hide the stem I wrap it tightly in cling film so that no sap from the peony can come into contact with the pudding.

Climbing plants like ivy and clematis are beautiful for draping over the base of a pudding stand, but both are poisonous and mustn't be eaten. They should never be placed on the actual pudding. In short, you have to be careful when you decorate with fresh flowers. Check with a reliable source whether or not your favourite plant or flower is edible. Use it as a guide for what can come into direct contact with the pudding, and what you should only use as table decorations.

UNMOULDING THE PUDDING

If there is anything that can make a cook sweat and become frantic, at least in my case, it's when the pudding refuses to come out of its mould. I've tried it a few times, jumping about on the spot, trying to get the wobbly dessert out of the mould! And I can reassure you that it is always successful. Over time I have developed a foolproof routine which I would suggest you copy. Before you begin, it's a good idea to get your serving plate ready as well as perhaps a container to serve as a water bath, and a clean tea towel to stand your mould and to dry it.

1. Start by making sure that the pudding has set as it should. Poke it with a finger – the pudding should feel firm, with a slightly rubbery resistance. As the pudding is made with soft-whipped cream, it contains little air, so a little can stick to your finger. But don't worry about it; nobody is going to see the bottom.

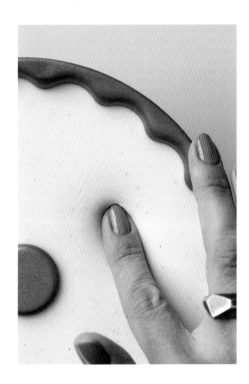

2. Fill the sink or your container with very hot water from the tap, and then dip the mould into the water all the way to the top (but don't let it overflow onto the pudding!) Count to 10 (or until you feel that the pudding has melted slightly around the edge of the mould), and lift the mould out of the water. If you've made an 'inverted pudding' using a fruit jelly, you only have to dip the mould in the water for about 5 seconds for it to melt, as jelly softens more quickly than set custard. If you've used agar-agar instead of gelatine to set the pudding, dip the mould into the water for a full 1–2 minutes as agar-agar sets pretty firmly and has a higher melting point.

3. Stand the mould on a tea towel, and wipe the outside with it lightly. Now you need to loosen the pudding from the edge of the mould. You can do this by gently pulling the pudding away from the edge of the mould with your finger, all the way around. If there is a chimney in the middle of the mould, then make sure to loosen the pudding from around that edge too. You can also use a small knife to carefully cut the pudding free, but this often leaves the pudding with unattractive edges.

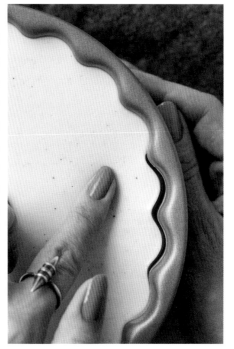

4. Take the serving plate, rinse it under the cold tap and pat it lightly with a tea towel so that it is not soaking wet but just moist. The moisture means that you will be able to easily manoeuvre the pudding and its mould on the plate if it does not land where it should once released from its mould. If you unmould a pudding onto a dry plate, it will stick like glue as soon as it comes into contact with the porcelain.

5. Cover the pudding mould with the plate and hold the two together with your hands – a palm under the mould and a palm over the plate. Quickly flip the mould and the plate over and make a downwards movement with them in the air so that the pudding is forced out of the mould with a slurp.

6. If the pudding refuses to budge, it may be because there is negative pressure inside the mould. If so, it may help to keep the mould slightly tilted, and perhaps to shake it lightly, first to one side and then to the other, so that it lets in a little air, while continuing to hold the mould and serving plate together. If the pudding STILL refuses to come out, then repeat all of the steps.

7. When you can feel and hear that the pudding has slid down inside the mould, then it's time to position it on the plate. Leave the mould on. Check that the pudding is centred on the plate. If not, gently slide the mould and its contents into the middle.

8. Now carefully lift the mould up off the pudding. Use both hands and lift it gently. And there you have it!

9. N.B. If the mould was left in the hot water for too long in step 2, there may be small puddles of melted custard (or juice lakes in the case of fruit jellies) on the pudding or the serving plate when you lift the mould off. If that happens, you can save the pudding by finding a straw, and secretly sucking up the puddles!

CLASSIC VANILLA BAVAROIS

Vanilla bavarois is to puddings what hollandaise is to sauces – a delicate base that can either be built on or that can stand alone. Then again, this wobbly dessert of egg yolks, milk, cream and vanilla is not just the foundation of all puddings – it is also the archetype of sweetness as we know it. This pudding is reminiscent of the crystallized vanilla parfait of village-hall parties, or the cream-filled éclairs from a trip to Paris, or the over-stiffened pastry cream at the local bakery.

Makes 1.2 litres/5 cups, serves 6–8

FOR THE BAVAROIS

7 leaves gelatine	2 vanilla pods
300 ml/1¼ cups whipping cream	8 egg yolks
400 ml/1⅜ cups whole milk	300 ml/1¼ cups whipping cream
160 g/¾ cup sugar	(for later addition)

Soak the gelatine in a large bowl of cold water.

Combine the first amount of cream with the milk and a couple of tablespoons of the sugar in a heavy-based saucepan together with the split vanilla pod and scrape out the seeds. Place over a low heat and heat until just short of boiling. Remove from the heat, cover the pan with a lid, and allow the vanilla to infuse in the milk and cream mixture for 10–15 minutes.

Beat the egg yolks and remaining sugar together in a large bowl.

Heat the vanilla-flavoured milk and cream mixture until just short of boiling. Then pour the hot mixture into the egg and sugar mixture while whisking vigorously. Transfer everything back into the pan and heat gently over a low heat while stirring with a silicone spatula or a wooden spoon until the temperature reaches 83–85°C (180–185°F). Do NOT allow the mixture to boil. The custard should be neither too runny nor too thick. Ideally, it should have a consistency that coats the back of a spoon (it should stick to the surface of the spatula or spoon without running off). (cont.)

Immediately remove the pan from the heat. Take the gelatine out of the water and squeeze out the excess liquid. Add it to the warm custard. Stir until the gelatine dissolves. Pass the custard through a sieve into a bowl. Allow it to cool slightly and then refrigerate. It should be cold in about 1–2 hours, and it may have set slightly around the edges of the bowl.

Beat the remaining cream into soft peaks. First fold a small amount into the chilled custard until smooth. Then gently fold in the rest of the soft-whipped cream.

Pour the bavarois into a suitable mould that has been rinsed in cold water. Refrigerate until firmly set, for at least 6 hours, or overnight.

See pages 34–37 for instructions on unmoulding the pudding.

Now you can decorate the pudding with whatever you want.

SUITABLE ACCOMPANIMENTS + DECORATIONS FOR
CLASSIC VANILLA BAVAROIS

- cherry sauce (see page 144) + maraschino cherries
- baked rhubarb with strawberries (see page 146) + fresh strawberries
- wild strawberries and lemon balm
- poached peaches (see pages 84–86) + edible flowers (see important information on page 33)
- salted caramel sauce (see page 143) + fresh raspberries

ALMOND PUDDING *with* AMARETTO

This was the first pudding I ever made, one I created in memory of the yellow powdered version of my childhood. It has lots of vanilla and a hint of almond from the amaretto. I have changed a couple of things in the recipe since the first time, so it is more sour and less creamy than version 1.0. If you ask me, this is how a genuine pudding should taste!

Makes 1.2 litres/5 cups, serves 6–8

FOR THE BAVAROIS

7 leaves gelatine

300 ml/1¼ cups whipping cream

400 ml/1⅜ cups whole milk

100 g/½ cup sugar

2 vanilla pods

8 egg yolks

75 ml/5 tbsp amaretto

300 ml/1¼ cups whipping cream
  (for later addition)

Soak the gelatine in a large bowl of cold water.

Combine the first amount of cream with the milk and a couple of tablespoons of the sugar in a heavy-based saucepan together with the split vanilla pod and scraped-out seeds. Place over a low heat and heat until just short of boiling. Remove from the heat, cover the pan with a lid, and allow the vanilla to infuse in the milk and cream mixture for 10–15 minutes.

Beat the egg yolks and remaining sugar together in a large bowl.

Heat the vanilla-flavoured milk and cream mixture until just short of boiling. Pour it hot into the egg and sugar mixture while whisking vigorously. Transfer everything back into the pan and heat gently over a low heat while stirring with a silicone spatula or a wooden spoon until the temperature reaches 83–85ºC (180–185°F). Do NOT allow the mixture to boil. The custard should be neither too runny nor too thick. Ideally, it should have a consistency that coats the back of a spoon (it should stick to the surface of the spatula or spoon without running off).

[cont.]

Immediately remove the pan from the heat. Take the gelatine out of the water and squeeze out the excess liquid. Add it to the warm custard. Stir until the gelatine dissolves. Add the amaretto and stir. Pass the custard through a sieve into a bowl. Allow it to cool slightly and then refrigerate. It should be cold in about 1–2 hours, and it may have set slightly around the edges of the bowl.

Beat the remaining cream into soft peaks. First fold a small amount into the chilled custard until smooth. Then gently fold in the rest of the soft-whipped cream.

Pour the bavarois into a suitable mould that has been rinsed in cold water. Refrigerate until firmly set, for at least 6 hours, or overnight.
See pages 34–37 for instructions on unmoulding the pudding.

Decorate the pudding with maraschino cherries if you're after an artificial look, or with fresh ones for something more natural. Serve the wobbly dessert with cherry sauce, stewed rhubarb, stewed blackcurrants with rum, or pickled blackberries.

SUITABLE ACCOMPANIMENTS + DECORATIONS FOR
ALMOND PUDDING *with* AMARETTO

- cherry sauce (see page 144) + maraschino cherries/fresh cherries
- baked rhubarb with strawberries (see page 146) + fresh strawberries
- stewed blackcurrants with rum (see page 154) + bunches of fresh blackcurrants
- wild strawberries and lemon balm
- salted caramel sauce (see page 143) + fresh raspberries
- baked apricots with pistachios (see page 145) + unsalted pistachios

RUM PUDDING *with* AN APPLE BASE

I created this pudding for a friend's birthday in the autumn, the perfect time to enjoy its slightly heavier taste. The apple base consists of a dense jellied apple compote, over which sits a bavarois made with dark rum, vanilla and brown sugar. This pudding is fabulous with salted caramel sauce, but if you don't have time to make it, maple syrup also makes a good accompaniment. You can also replace the rum with Calvados to bring out the apple flavour. Naturally, you can always leave out the apple base and just make the pudding – I promise you that it's a very good version of a rum bavarois.

Makes 2 litres/8 ½ cups, serves 12

FOR THE RUM BAVAROIS

10 leaves gelatine

10 egg yolks

180 g/⅞ cup brown sugar

550 ml/2 cups + 3 tbsp whole milk

400 ml/1⅜ cups whipping cream

¼ tsp sea salt

1 vanilla pod

100 ml/⅜ cup dark rum

350 ml/1½ cups whipping cream
 (for later addition)

FOR THE APPLE BASE

4 leaves gelatine

1 kg/2 lbs apples

50 ml/3 tbsp water

1 vanilla pod

75–125 g/⅓–⅔ cup sugar

Soak the gelatine for the rum bavarois in a large bowl of cold water.

Set aside a couple of tablespoons of sugar and beat the rest together with the egg yolks in a large mixing bowl.

Combine the milk, the first amount of cream and the reserved sugar in a heavy-

based saucepan together with the split vanilla pod and scraped-out seeds. Place over a low heat until just short of boiling.

Pour the hot milk and cream mixture into the egg and sugar mixture, whisking vigorously. Transfer everything back into the pan and heat gently over a low heat while stirring with a silicone spatula or a wooden spoon until the temperature reaches 83–85°C (180–185°F). Do NOT allow the mixture to boil. The custard should be neither too runny nor too thick. Ideally, it should have a consistency that coats the back of a spoon (it should stick to the surface of the spatula or spoon without running off).

Immediately remove the pan from the heat. Take the gelatine out of the water and squeeze out the excess liquid. Add it to the warm custard. Stir until the gelatine dissolves. Stir in the rum. Pass the custard through a sieve into a bowl. Allow it to cool slightly and then refrigerate. It should be cold in about 2 hours, and it may have set slightly around the edges of the bowl.

Beat the remaining cream into soft peaks. First fold a small amount into the chilled custard until smooth. Then gently fold in the rest of the soft-whipped cream.

Pour the bavarois into a suitable mould that has been rinsed in cold water. Remember to leave a space of 2–3 cm from the top of the mould for the apple base. Refrigerate until firmly set, for at least 6 hours, or overnight.

Peel and core the apples. Chop them coarsely into pieces and put them in a heavy-based saucepan with the water. Split the vanilla pod, scrape out the seeds and mash them together with a little sugar using the flat of a knife to separate the seeds. Add the vanilla pod and the sugar and seed mixture to the pan. Cover the pan with a lid and steam the apples over a low heat until completely tender (about 20–30 minutes, depending on the variety and ripeness). Add a little more water if necessary.

Meanwhile, soak the gelatine for the apple base in a bowl of cold water for about 10 minutes.

Add sugar to the compote (depending on the flavour and tartness of the apples), and beat with a whisk until smooth.

Measure out 400 ml/1³/₈ cups of the warm compote into a bowl, and keep any left over for an apple pie or for breakfast. Add the softened gelatine to the warm compote and blend until smooth with a hand-held blender. Leave the compote to cool to room temperature.

Spread the compote over the set pudding with a spatula or spoon, and put the pudding back in the refrigerator for at least 3 hours or until the apple compote has set.

See pages 34–37 for instructions on unmoulding the pudding.

Decorate the pudding with dried apple rings or small crab apples.

Tip
You can leave out the apple base and make a chocolate pudding for children, decorated with chopped dark chocolate (or add a little chocolate to the bavarois when it begins to set) and serve it with salted caramel sauce.

SUITABLE ACCOMPANIMENTS + DECORATIONS FOR
RUM PUDDING *with* AN APPLE BASE

- extra apple compote (see page 149) + dried apple rings
- whipped cream + fresh crab apples
- salted caramel sauce (see page 143) + dark chocolate
- salted caramel sauce (see page 143) + salted caramel popcorn (see page 111)

COFFEE AND CARAMEL PUDDING

I've always liked coffee desserts. I have also always loved crème caramel. This pudding is a kind of fusion of the two, which I first made while writing the book Foodie. *I have since modified the recipe to make it even more creamy and wobbly. The basic ingredient for this pudding is a caramel syrup made from caramelized sugar and good strong coffee. The latter is crucial for its flavour, and I always use coffee beans from my favourite roaster, The Coffee Collective, who ship from their website. I brew the equivalent of a cafetière of extra-strong coffee (I usually use 60 g/¾ cup of coffee beans to 1 litre/4 cups of water, but here I use 30 g/6 tbsp for 400 ml/1⅝ cups) – but if you don't have a cafetière or coffee press, you can easily make it in a machine with the same amount of beans and water.*

Makes 1.2 litres/5 cups, serves 6–8

FOR THE COFFEE AND CARAMEL SYRUP

30 g/6 tbsp freshly ground coffee
   beans

400 ml/1⅝ cups boiling water
6 leaves gelatine
100 g/½ cup sugar

FOR THE BAVAROIS

8 egg yolks
70 g/⅓ cup sugar
300 ml/1¼ cups whole milk

200 ml/⅞ cup whipping cream
250 ml/1 cup whipping cream
(for later addition)

Start by brewing a small cafetière of strong coffee. Coarsely grind high-quality, freshly roasted coffee beans and put them into the cafetière. Boil the water and leave to stand for 1 minute. Pour the water over the ground coffee in the cafetière and leave to infuse for 4 minutes. Stir in the grounds, which will have risen to the top as a foam. Slowly push the plunger down to the bottom of the beaker.

Soak the gelatine for the syrup in a large bowl of cold water.

Now make the syrup. Sprinkle the sugar into a dry sauté pan or frying pan and melt it into a bubbling light golden-brown caramel. Remove the pan from the heat and carefully pour the coffee in a little at a time. Be very careful, as it will splatter. Re-

duce the coffee syrup by half, to about 200 ml/⅞ cup. Transfer the syrup to a bowl or a measuring jug with a spout, and leave it to cool a little.

Take the gelatine out of the water, squeeze out the excess liquid, and add it to the warm caramel syrup. Stir until the gelatine is dissolved, then leave the syrup to stand.

Set aside a couple of tablespoons of sugar and beat the rest together with the egg yolks in a large mixing bowl.

Combine the milk, the first amount of cream and the reserved sugar in a heavy-based saucepan. Place over a low heat until just short of boiling.

Pour the hot milk and cream mixture into the egg and sugar mixture, whisking vigorously. Transfer everything back into the pan and heat gently over a low heat while stirring with a silicone spatula or a wooden spoon until the temperature reaches 83–85°C (180–185°F). Do NOT allow the mixture to boil. The custard should be neither too runny nor too thick. Ideally, it should have a consistency that coats the back of a spoon (it should stick to the surface of the spatula or spoon without running off).

Immediately remove the pan from the heat. Add the coffee and caramel syrup and whisk it into the custard. Pass the custard through a sieve into a bowl. Allow it to cool slightly and then refrigerate. It should be cold in about 1–2 hours, and it may have set slightly around the edges of the bowl.

Beat the remaining cream into soft peaks. First fold a small amount into the chilled custard until smooth. Then gently fold in the rest of the soft-whipped cream.

Pour the bavarois into a suitable mould that has been rinsed in cold water. Refrigerate until firmly set, for at least 6 hours, or overnight.

See pages 34–37 for instructions on unmoulding the pudding.

Decorate the pudding with whipped cream and, if you are feeling adventurous, whole coffee beans. Bear in mind that they should not be eaten. Serve with extra whipped cream on the side.

SUITABLE ACCOMPANIMENTS + DECORATIONS FOR
COFFEE AND CARAMEL PUDDING

- whipped cream swirls + whole coffee beans
- salted caramel sauce (see page 143) + dark chocolate

VIOLET PUDDING

I have a weakness for anything flavoured with violet, a taste which, unfortunately, is not common. Violet tea, violet macarons, and of course, violet pudding. The violet syrup that I use to flavour this pudding is from the French company Monin. You can buy it online and have it delivered. You could also choose to leave out the violet and instead turn this into a recipe for a fine, pale yellow elderflower pudding by switching the violet syrup for undiluted elderflower cordial.

Makes 1.2 litres/5 cups, serves 6–8

FOR THE BAVAROIS

6 leaves gelatine

8 egg yolks

50 g/¼ cup sugar

300 ml/1¼ cups whole milk

300 ml/1¼ cups whipping cream

150 ml/⅔ cup Monin violet syrup

Juice of ½–1 lemon

300 ml/1¼ cups whipping cream
  (for later addition)

Soak the gelatine in a large bowl of cold water.

Set aside about 1 tablespoon of sugar and beat the rest together with the egg yolks in a large mixing bowl.

Combine the milk, the first amount of cream and the reserved sugar in a heavy-based saucepan. Place over a low heat until just short of boiling.

Pour the hot milk and cream mixture into the egg and sugar mixture, whisking vigorously. Transfer everything back into the pan and heat gently over a low heat while stirring with a silicone spatula or a wooden spoon until the temperature reaches 83–85°C (180–185°F). Do NOT allow the mixture to boil. The custard should be neither too runny nor too thick. Ideally, it should have a consistency that coats the back of a spoon (it should stick to the surface of the spatula or spoon without running off).

Immediately remove the pan from the heat. Take the gelatine out of the water and

squeeze out the excess liquid. Add it to the warm custard. Stir until the gelatine dissolves. Add the violet syrup and the lemon juice. Pass the custard through a sieve into a bowl. Allow it to cool slightly and then refrigerate. It should be cold in about 1–2 hours, and it may have set slightly around the edges of the bowl.

Beat the remaining cream into soft peaks. First fold a small amount into the chilled custard until smooth. Then gently fold in the rest of the soft-whipped cream.

Pour the bavarois into a suitable mould that has been rinsed in cold water. Refrigerate until firmly set, for at least 6 hours, or overnight.

See pages 34-37 for instructions on unmoulding the pudding.

Decorate the pudding with fresh violets or violet leaves, if you can find them, and perhaps bunches of fresh blackcurrants.

Tip

Replace the violet syrup with the same amount of undiluted elderflower cordial to make an elderflower pudding. Decorate the elderflower pudding with fresh elderflowers and serve with gooseberry sauce (see page 151) or fresh strawberries.

SUITABLE ACCOMPANIMENTS + DECORATIONS FOR
VIOLET PUDDING

- fresh blackcurrants, stewed blackcurrants with rum (see page 154) + lilacs or other edible flowers (see important information on page 33)
- salted liquorice syrup from John Bulow (www.scandikitchen.co.uk) + fresh or candied violets and violet leaves
- blackberry sauce (see page 153) + fresh blackberries

COCOA PUDDING

This is the simplest pudding to make, and a favourite with children. While most of the puddings I make are bavarois (put more simply, a custard aerated with whipped cream and set with gelatine), this pudding is quite simply a chocolate cream jelly, or a cocoa cream jelly, to be more precise. Therefore, I would recommend the use of a high-quality, pure cocoa powder from Scharffen Berger or Valrhona, for instance. If you like, you can flavour the pudding with orange flower water, maraschino liqueur or orange peel. You can also replace the water in the recipe with brandy, for a truly grown-up pudding.

Makes 1 litre/4 cups, serves 6

FOR THE COCOA CREAM JELLY

7 leaves gelatine
800 ml/3⅓ cups whipping cream
170 g/¾ cup sugar
100 ml/⅜ cup water

80 g/¾ cup high-quality cocoa powder (I use Scharffen Berger)
About 2 tablespoons orange flower water or maraschino liqueur

Soak the gelatine in a large bowl of cold water.
Bring the cream to the boil in a heavy-based saucepan with a couple of tablespoons of the sugar. Combine the remaining sugar and cocoa powder in a small bowl. Pour 100 ml/⅜ cup of boiling water from a kettle into the sugar and cocoa mixture, and stir so that it melts a little. Pour this mixture into the hot cream. Cook the cocoa cream for a few minutes until the sugar is completely dissolved.
Remove the pan from the heat. Take the gelatine out of the water, squeeze out the excess liquid, and add it to the warm cocoa cream. Stir until the gelatine dissolves. Add the orange flower water, liqueur or other flavouring – you may prefer to stick to simple cocoa.

Pour the cocoa cream straight into a suitable mould that has been rinsed in cold water. If you have individual moulds, use them. There should be enough for 6–8

moulds, depending on their size. Carefully place the very liquid pudding in the refrigerator and allow it to set for at least 6 hours, or overnight.

See pages 34–37 for instructions on unmoulding the pudding.

Decorate the pudding with whipped cream and maraschino cherries for a kitsch look, or with fresh fruit if you're after a more natural appearance.

SUITABLE ACCOMPANIMENTS + DECORATIONS FOR
COCOA PUDDING

- whipped cream swirls + maraschino cherries, chocolate or cocoa nibs
- orange salad with orange flower water and cocoa nibs (see page 152) + sliced kumquats
- crème anglaise (see page 147) + orange slices
- whipped cream swirls + pineapple and cherry cream

CHOCOLATE PUDDING

No book on puddings would be complete without a chocolate pudding! Here is a simple wobbly pudding that isn't too sweet, and with the pure and subtle flavour of chocolate and cream. I use Valrhona's high-quality Caraïbe chocolate, which has a hint of bitterness. This pudding is best served with a passion fruit compote and banana. If you decide to use a different brand of chocolate, make sure to find one with a roughly equivalent percentage of cocoa. It's not that I'm a percentage snob, but because the amount of cocoa solids in relation to the amount of cocoa butter in the chocolate affects the consistency of the pudding.

Makes 1.5 litres/6 cups, serves 8–10

FOR THE BAVAROIS

6 leaves gelatine

8 egg yolks

160 g/¾ cup sugar

400 ml/1⅜ cups whole milk

300 ml/1¼ cups whipping cream

150 g/6 oz dark chocolate, Valrhona Caraïbe (64% cocoa)

300 ml/1¼ cups whipping cream (for later addition)

Soak the gelatine in a large bowl of cold water.

Set aside a couple of tablespoons of sugar and beat the rest together with the egg yolks in a large mixing bowl.

Combine the milk, the first amount of cream and the reserved sugar in a heavy-based saucepan. Place over a low heat until just short of boiling.

Pour the hot milk and cream mixture into the egg and sugar mixture, whisking vigorously. Transfer everything back into the pan and heat gently over a low heat while stirring with a silicone spatula or a wooden spoon until the temperature reaches 83–85°C (180–185°F). Do NOT allow the mixture to boil. The custard should be neither too runny nor too thick. Ideally, it should have a consistency that coats the back of a spoon (it should stick to the surface of the spatula or spoon without

running off).

Immediately remove the pan from the heat. Take the gelatine out of the water and squeeze out the excess liquid. Add it to the warm custard. Stir until the gelatine dissolves. Pass the custard through a sieve into a bowl.

Chop up the chocolate with a bread knife and melt in a bowl in a bain-marie or in the microwave.

Incorporate the melted chocolate into the warm custard. If the mixture seems to separate a little, blend with a hand-held blender. Don't overdo it, just blend gently, and only enough so that the chocolate bits melt evenly throughout the custard.

Refrigerate. It should be cold in about 1–2 hours, and it may have set slightly around the edges of the bowl.

Beat the remaining cream into soft peaks. First fold a small amount into the chilled custard until smooth. Then gently fold in the rest of the soft-whipped cream.

Pour the bavarois into a suitable mould that has been rinsed in cold water. Refrigerate until firmly set, for at least 6 hours, or overnight.

See pages 34–37 for instructions on turning the pudding out of the mould.

Decorate the pudding with swirls of whipped cream, cocoa nibs and perhaps maraschino cherries or a passion fruit compote and fresh bananas, depending on the occasion.

Tip

Make a wonderfully childish 'surprise chocolate pudding' by studding the bottom of the pudding with mini cream puffs bought or homemade when it is half set. Push the cream puffs into the pudding so that their bottoms are flush with the surface of the pudding.

SUITABLE ACCOMPANIMENTS + DECORATIONS FOR
CHOCOLATE PUDDING

- banana and passion fruit compote (see page 142) + whipped cream swirls and cocoa nibs
- salted caramel sauce (see page 143) + banana slices
- chocolate sauce (see page 150) + maraschino cherries
- baked apricots with pistachios (see page 145) + whipped cream swirls and un-salted pistachios

WHITE CHOCOLATE
and JASMINE TEA PUDDING

The pairing of green tea and white chocolate has become a classic contemporary dessert, and a combination I just had to try in pudding form. I chose to use jasmine green tea, which is quite easy to get hold of in most tea shops, but if you have an Earl Grey green, which is flavoured with bergamot, that will also work well. The same is true for matcha tea; however, this should not be added to the cream when making the custard, but simply mixed into the finished bavarois. Serve the pudding with fresh or sugared raspberries.

Makes 1.5 litres/6 cups, serves 8-10

FOR THE BAVAROIS

6 leaves gelatine

500 ml/2 cups whole milk

200 ml/⅞ cup whipping cream

160 g/¾ cup sugar

8 egg yolks

20 g/¾ oz loose leaf jasmine green tea

130 g/5 oz white chocolate, such as Valrhona
  Ivoire (35% cocoa)

300 ml/1¼ cups whipping cream (for later
  addition)

Soak the gelatine in a large bowl of cold water.

Combine the milk, first amount of cream and a couple of tablespoons of the sugar in a heavy-based saucepan. Place over a low heat until just short of boiling. Add the tea leaves, remove the pan from the heat, cover with a lid and leave the tea to infuse in the milk and cream mixture for 10–15 minutes. Pass the cream mixture through a sieve into a bowl to separate the tea leaves. Their job is done now.

Beat the egg yolks and remaining sugar together in a large bowl.

Heat the tea-flavoured milk and cream mixture once again to just short of boiling. Pour the hot milk and cream mixture into the egg and sugar mixture, whisking vigorously. Transfer everything back into the pan and heat gently over a low heat while stirring with a silicone spatula or a wooden spoon until the temperature

reaches 83–85°C (180–185°F). Do NOT allow the mixture to boil. The custard should be neither too runny nor too thick. Ideally, it should have a consistency that coats the back of a spoon (it should stick to the surface of the spatula or spoon without running off).

Immediately remove the pan from the heat. Take the gelatine out of the water and squeeze out the excess liquid. Add it to the warm custard. Stir until the gelatine dissolves. Pass the custard through a sieve into a bowl.

Chop up the chocolate with a bread knife and melt in a bowl in a bain-marie or in the microwave.

Incorporate the melted chocolate into the warm custard. If the mixture seems to separate a little, blend with a hand-held blender. Don't overdo it, just blend gently, and only enough so that the chocolate bits melt evenly throughout the custard.

Refrigerate. It should be cold in about 1–2 hours, and it may have set slightly around the edges of the bowl.

Beat the remaining cream into soft peaks. First fold a small amount into the chilled custard until smooth. Then gently fold in the rest of the soft-whipped cream.

Pour the bavarois into a suitable mould that has been rinsed in cold water. Refrigerate until firmly set, for at least 6 hours, or overnight.

See pages 34–37 for instructions on unmoulding the pudding.

It would look lovely to decorate the pudding with fresh jasmine blossoms, but they may not be easy to find, and while the closest thing to it, mock orange, may grow in a garden near you, it's poisonous. So, if you are not sure what you're doing, just decorate the table around the pudding.

SUITABLE ACCOMPANIMENTS + DECORATIONS FOR
WHITE CHOCOLATE and JASMINE TEA PUDDING

- shaken raspberries with rose water (see page 144) + fresh raspberries
- shaken redcurrants (see page 150) + redcurrant leaves

ROSE GERANIUM PUDDING
with RASPBERRIES

Rose geranium is my favourite herb for making desserts. With its notes of citrus and roses, this green plant is just made for adding its flavour to puddings, creams and compotes. I don't mean the heavy, sickly sweet perfume you find in taxis in summer, but a subtle, understated scent that really just works. If you serve rose geranium pudding with shaken raspberries or stewed rhubarb, you will make people very, very happy.

Makes 1.5 litres/6 cups, serves 8-10

FOR THE BAVAROIS

300 g/10 oz frozen or fresh raspberries (for 150 ml/⅔ cup raspberry juice)

7 leaves gelatine

400 ml/1⅜ cups whole milk

300 ml/1¼ cups whipping cream

8 rose geranium leaves (see tip page 74)

10 egg yolks

190 g/scant 1 cup sugar

300 ml/1¼ cups whipping cream (for later addition)

Put the raspberries in a saucepan, and leave to stand until they soften. If you're using fresh raspberries, sprinkle with a few tablespoons of the weighed-out sugar. Give the berries a quick boil, and then pour them into a sieve over a bowl to collect the juice, which you will need for the recipe. This should give you 150 ml/⅔ cup of raspberry juice. Mash the berries a little so they release all their juice. If there isn't quite enough juice, make up for the shortfall with lemon juice.

Soak the gelatine in a large bowl of cold water.

Combine the milk, first amount of cream and a couple of tablespoons of the sugar in a heavy-based saucepan with the rose geranium leaves. Place over a low heat until just short of boiling. Remove the pan from the heat, cover with a lid, and allow the leaves to infuse in the milk and cream mixture for 10–15 minutes.

Beat the egg yolks and remaining sugar together in a large bowl.

[cont.]

Heat the leaf-infused milk and cream mixture once again to just short of boiling.

Pour the hot milk and cream mixture into the egg and sugar mixture, whisking vigorously. Transfer everything back into the pan and heat gently over a low heat while stirring with a silicone spatula or a wooden spoon until the temperature reaches 83–85°C (180–185°F). Do NOT allow the mixture to boil. The custard should be neither too runny nor too thick. Ideally, it should have a consistency that coats the back of a spoon (it should stick to the surface of the spatula or spoon without running off).

Immediately remove the pan from the heat. Take the gelatine out of the water and squeeze out the excess liquid. Add it to the warm custard. Stir until the gelatine dissolves. Add the 150 ml of raspberry juice, and then pass the custard through a sieve into a bowl.

Refrigerate. It should be cold in about 1–2 hours, and it may have set slightly around the edges of the bowl.

Beat the remaining cream into soft peaks. First fold a small amount into the chilled custard until smooth. Then gently fold in the rest of the soft-whipped cream.

Pour the bavarois into a suitable mould that has been rinsed in cold water. Refrigerate until set, for at least 6 hours, or overnight.

See pages 34–37 for instructions on unmoulding the pudding.

Decorate the pudding with roses and geranium leaves.

Tip

Rose geranium is a wonderful herb for use in desserts, especially those made with rhubarb, citrus, roses and raspberries. The leaves of this fragrant potted plant give off an unmistakable scent of citrus and rose, because they contain the same essential oils (geraniol and citronellol) as roses. I buy my geraniums at the florist's; they cost next to nothing and stand fragrantly in my kitchen window. They are easy to care for, and it is normal for them to shed a few leaves quite often. When choosing a geranium for use in cooking, sample the scent by rubbing the leaves between your fingers – they have a very strong fragrance.

SUITABLE ACCOMPANIMENTS + DECORATIONS FOR
ROSE GERANIUM PUDDING *with* RASPBERRIES

- baked rhubarb with strawberries (see page 146) + rose geranium leaves
- shaken raspberries with rose water (see page 144) + fresh raspberries
- raspberry sauce (see blackberry sauce, page 153) + fresh raspberries

APRICOT *and* AMARETTO PUDDING

You know when certain ingredients appear on a menu and you just have to choose that dish? That's how I feel about apricots. They trump everything else, even cherry and rhubarb, perhaps because I so rarely encounter these small aromatic stone fruits. That's why I made this pudding. It has a shot of amaretto, because the flavours of almond and apricot are so closely related that not only do they complement each other, one really brings out the other. I really hope you decide to make it.

Makes 1.5 litres/6 cups, serves 8–10

FOR THE APRICOT PURÉE

400 g/14 oz ripe apricots

100 ml/⅜ cup water

50 g/¼ cup sugar

Juice of ½ lemon

50 ml/3 tbsp amaretto

FOR THE BAVAROIS

8 leaves gelatine

8 egg yolks

160 g/¾ cup sugar

400 ml/1⅜ cups whole milk

300 ml/1¼ cups whipping cream

300 ml/1¼ cups whipping cream
  (for later addition)

Wash the apricots, cut them open and remove the stones. Cut the flesh into wedges. Combine the water and sugar in a small saucepan and heat until the sugar melts. Add the apricots to the sugar syrup and simmer for 10 minutes. Add the lemon juice and amaretto and blend the mixture into a fine purée.

Soak the gelatine in a large bowl of cold water.

Set aside a couple of tablespoons of sugar and beat the rest together with the egg yolks in a large mixing bowl.

Combine the milk, first amount of cream and the reserved sugar in a heavy-based saucepan. Place over a low heat until just short of boiling.

[cont.]

Pour the hot milk and cream mixture into the egg and sugar mixture, whisking vigorously. Transfer everything back into the pan and heat gently over a low heat while stirring with a silicone spatula or a wooden spoon until the temperature reaches 83–85°C (180–185°F). Do NOT allow the mixture to boil. The custard should be neither too runny nor too thick. Ideally, it should have a consistency that coats the back of a spoon (it should stick to the surface of the spatula or spoon without running off).

Immediately remove the custard from the heat. Take the gelatine out of the water and squeeze out the excess liquid. Add it to the warm custard. Stir until the gelatine dissolves. Pass the custard through a sieve into a bowl. Add the apricot purée and blend with a hand-held blender until smooth. Pass the custard through the sieve again to remove any remaining pieces of orange apricot skin.

Refrigerate. It should be cold in about 1–2 hours, and it may have set slightly around the edges of the bowl.

Beat the remaining cream into soft peaks. First fold a small amount into the chilled custard until smooth. Then gently fold in the rest of the soft-whipped cream.

Pour the bavarois into a suitable mould that has been rinsed in cold water. Refrigerate until firmly set, for at least 6 hours, or overnight.

See pages 34–37 for instructions on unmoulding the pudding.

Decorate the pudding with apricot halves and blanched almonds or unsalted pistachios.

SUITABLE ACCOMPANIMENTS + DECORATIONS FOR
APRICOT *and* AMARETTO PUDDING

- fresh apricots + unsalted pistachios / blanched almonds
- baked apricots with pistachios (see page 145) + whipped cream and unsalted pistachios
- cherry sauce (see page 144) + small macaroons

VANILLA BAVAROIS
with
RHUBARB JELLY

If, like me, you have a penchant for everything rhubarb, then you'll love this pudding, which is inspired by the cheesecake I typically make for my birthday every year. This year, however, I made this pudding. It has the most beautiful crowning layer of rose geranium-flavoured rhubarb jelly with very special notes of rose and citrus. Potted geraniums are easy to find at the florist's (also see the tips on page 33).

Makes 1.5 litres/6 cups, serves 8–10

FOR THE BAKED RHUBARB

About 1 kg/2 lbs rhubarb (cleaned weight)

375 g/1¾ cups sugar

3–4 rose geranium leaves

FOR THE RHUBARB JELLY

3 leaves gelatine

Baked rhubarb (drained)

300 ml/1¼ cups baked rhubarb cooking liquid

FOR THE BAVAROIS

7 leaves gelatine

400 ml/1⅜ cups whole milk

300 ml/1¼ cups whipping cream

160 g/¾ cup sugar

2 vanilla pods

8 egg yolks

300 ml/1¼ cups whipping cream
  (for later addition)

Preheat the oven to 200°C (400°F, gas 6). Clean the rhubarb and cut into small pieces, then combine in an ovenproof dish with the sugar and whole geranium leaves. Bake for about 20 minutes. Gently turn the rhubarb over once while baking. Take the dish out of the oven and let the liquid in the dish cool to room temperature. Transfer the rhubarb to a sieve over a bowl. Leave it to drain and collect the cooking liquid.

Soak the gelatine for the rhubarb jelly in a bowl of cold water. The rhubarb should yield about 300 ml/1¼ cups of liquid (if there is too little, you can make up for the shortfall with a little water; if there's too much, you can save it as a delicious addition to your breakfast). Pour a little of the liquid into a small saucepan. Take the gelatine out of the water, squeeze out the excess liquid, and add it to the warm rhubarb cooking liquid. Stir until the gelatine dissolves and then blend it into the rest of the cooking liquid.

Now pour the jelly mixture into a 1.5–1.7-litre mould and leave it in the fridge until it starts to set around the edge of the mould. It shouldn't take too long as there's only a small amount. Once the jelly begins to set, you can add the rhubarb pieces. Do not use all the baked rhubarb – only about a third, depending on the mould – as there needs to be space to fill the rest of the mould with bavarois. There should be 1 part rhubarb jelly to 2–3 parts bavarois. Take the tender pieces of rhubarb and gently press them one at a time into the partly set jelly. If the jelly suddenly becomes too solid to insert the rhubarb pieces, simply fill a container with very hot water and dip the mould into it briefly to melt the jelly. The task should now become easier.

Return the mould to the refrigerator. The jelly needs to set completely, which should take 2–3 hours.

Soak the gelatine for the bavarois in a large bowl of cold water.

Combine the milk, first amount of cream and a couple of tablespoons of the sugar in a heavy-based saucepan together with the split vanilla pods and scraped-out seeds. Place over a low heat until just short of boiling. Remove from the heat, cover the pan with a lid, and allow the vanilla to infuse in the milk and cream mixture for 10–15 minutes.

Beat the egg yolks and remaining sugar together in a large bowl.

Heat the vanilla-flavoured milk and cream mixture until just short of boiling. Pour it hot into the egg and sugar mixture while whisking vigorously. Transfer everything back into the pan and heat gently over a low heat while stirring with a silicone spatula or a wooden spoon until the temperature reaches 83–85°C (180–185°F). Do NOT allow the mixture to boil. The custard should be neither too runny nor too thick. Ideally, it should have a consistency that coats the back of a spoon (it should stick to the surface of the spatula or spoon without running off).

Immediately remove the pan from the heat. Take the gelatine out of the water and squeeze out the excess liquid. Add it to the warm custard. Stir until the gelatine dissolves. Pass the custard through a sieve into a bowl. Allow it to cool slightly and then refrigerate. It should be cold in about 1–2 hours, and it may have set slightly around the edges of the bowl.

Beat the remaining cream into soft peaks. First fold a small amount into the chilled custard until smooth. Then gently fold in the rest of the soft-whipped cream.

Pour the bavarois into the mould with the rhubarb jelly and refrigerate until completely set, for at least 6 hours, or overnight.

See pages 34–37 for instructions on unmoulding the pudding.

Decorate the pudding with fresh geranium leaves before serving.

SUITABLE ACCOMPANIMENTS + DECORATIONS FOR
VANILLA BAVAROIS with RHUBARB JELLY

- leftover baked rhubarb + geranium leaves
- fresh strawberries

ALMOND PUDDING
with A PEACH CROWN

Doesn't this sound lovely? This is a pudding imbued with my favourite almond flavouring, amaretto, and crowned with a layer of vanilla-poached peaches in jelly. The peaches are sliced so that they fit inside the fluting found on many pudding moulds, and hopefully on yours! Choose highly fragrant and very ripe peaches. They won't be any good if they're hard.

Makes 1.5 litres/6 cups, serves 8–10

FOR THE PEACH CROWN

4 leaves gelatine

5 ripe peaches

1 litre/4 cups water

300 g/1½ cups sugar

1 vanilla pod

The juice of ½ a lemon

FOR THE BAVAROIS

7 leaves gelatine

300 ml/1¼ cups whipping cream

400 ml/1⅜ cups whole milk

100 g/½ cup sugar

8 egg yolks

75 ml/5 tbsp amaretto

300 ml/1¼ cups whipping cream

(for later addition)

Soak the gelatine for the peach crown in a bowl of cold water.

Put the peaches into a heat-resistant bowl, pour boiling water over them and leave to stand for 15 seconds. Transfer to a sieve and rinse with a little cold water. Peel the peaches with a paring knife, cut them open and remove the stones.

Pour the litre of water into a deep frying pan or a wide saucepan and add the sugar. Add the split vanilla pod and scraped-out seeds. Cook until the sugar melts, and then carefully place the peach halves in the syrup with the rounded side facing upwards. Poach the peaches over a low heat for about 15 minutes.

[cont.]

Transfer the peaches to a container and allow them to cool slightly.

Dissolve the gelatine for the peach crown in 300 ml/1¼ cups of the syrup. Add the lemon juice and strain through a sieve. Pour a shallow layer (1–2 cm) of the jelly mixture into a suitable pudding mould. Refrigerate until the mixture begins to set slightly around the edges. Set aside the rest of the jelly mixture.

Thinly slice the poached peaches with a sharp knife. Insert the slices into the partly set jelly at the bottom of the fluted pudding mould, arranging them to fit inside the grooves. Refrigerate for 25–35 minutes, or until the peaches and syrup just begin to hold their shape inside the mould. Spoon the rest of the jelly mixture over the peaches. Do this carefully, one spoon at a time, so as not to disturb the arrangement. Return the mould to the refrigerator. Place any remaining peach slices in a bowl and cover with a little of the syrup from the pan. You can serve them as an accompaniment.

Now make the bavarois while the jelly sets.

Soak the gelatine in a large bowl of cold water.

Set aside a couple of tablespoons of sugar and beat the rest together with the egg yolks in a large mixing bowl.

Combine the milk, first amount of cream and the reserved sugar in a heavy-based saucepan. Place over a low heat until just short of boiling.

Pour the hot milk and cream mixture into the egg and sugar mixture, whisking vigorously. Transfer everything back into the pan and heat gently over a low heat while stirring with a silicone spatula or a wooden spoon until the temperature reaches 83–85°C (180–185°F). Do NOT allow the mixture to boil. The custard should be neither too runny nor too thick. Ideally, it should have a consistency that coats the back of a spoon (it should stick to the surface of the spatula or spoon without running off).

Immediately remove the pan from the heat. Take the gelatine out of the water and squeeze out the excess liquid. Add it to the warm custard. Stir until the gelatine dissolves. Stir in the amaretto. Pass the custard through a sieve into a bowl. Allow it to cool slightly and then refrigerate. It should be cold in about 1–2 hours, and it may have set slightly around the edges of the bowl.

Beat the remaining cream into soft peaks. First fold a small amount into the chilled custard until smooth. Then gently fold in the rest of the soft-whipped cream.

Pour the bavarois into the mould over on the already-set peach crown, and refrigerate until firmly set, for at least 6 hours, or overnight.

See pages 34–37 for instructions on unmoulding the pudding.

This pudding looks beautiful on its own, but you can also decorate it with fresh raspberries around the edge, like a peach Melba.

SUITABLE ACCOMPANIMENTS + DECORATIONS FOR
ALMOND PUDDING with A PEACH CROWN

- leftover poached peaches + fresh raspberries
- crème anglaise (see page 147)
- shaken raspberries with rose water (see page 144) + white roses, carnations or peonies (see important information on page 33)

BUTTERMILK PUDDING

This is a very summery pudding that tastes of buttermilk, vanilla and lemon. Such things as fresh berries and compotes, and vanilla biscuits for added crunch, all taste wonderful with this pudding. I have omitted aeration with whipped cream, in order to create a dense and smooth consistency. Buttermilk pudding is a classic, and I have come across it in multiple versions, including without eggs, which would actually be a buttermilk panna cotta. And while that would certainly be delicious, this sort of pudding cries out for the taste of custard made with egg yolks!

Makes 1.5 litres/6 cups, serves 8–10

FOR THE BAVAROIS

8 leaves gelatine

600 ml/2½ cups whipping cream

180 g/⅞ cup sugar

2 vanilla pods

1½–2 organic lemons (for
   100 ml/⅜ cup juice)

12 egg yolks

500 ml/2 cups buttermilk

Soak the gelatine in a large bowl of cold water.

Combine the cream, a couple of tablespoons of the sugar, the split vanilla pods and scraped-out seeds, and strips of zest from one lemon in a heavy-based saucepan. Place over a low heat until just short of boiling. Remove from the heat, cover the pan with a lid, and allow the vanilla and lemon zest to infuse in the cream for 10–15 minutes.

Beat the egg yolks and remaining sugar together in a large bowl.

Heat the flavoured cream until just short of boiling. Pour it hot into the egg and sugar mixture while whisking vigorously. Transfer everything back into the pan and heat gently over a low heat while stirring with a silicone spatula or a wooden spoon until the temperature reaches 83–85°C (180–185°F). Do NOT allow the mixture to boil. The custard should be neither too runny nor too thick. Ideally, it should have a consistency that coats the back of a spoon (it should stick to the surface of the spatula or

spoon without running off).

Immediately remove the pan from the heat. Take the gelatine out of the water and squeeze out the excess liquid. Add it to the warm custard. Stir until the gelatine dissolves. Add the buttermilk and lemon juice, and pass the custard through a sieve into a bowl. Allow it to cool slightly and then refrigerate. It should be cold in about 1–2 hours, and it may have set slightly around the edges of the bowl.

Stir to distribute the vanilla seeds evenly.

Pour the bavarois into a suitable mould that has been rinsed in cold water. Refrigerate until firmly set, for at least 6 hours, or overnight.

See pages 34–37 for instructions on unmoulding the pudding.

Decorate the pudding with fruits or berries, depending on the occasion.

SUITABLE ACCOMPANIMENTS + DECORATIONS FOR
BUTTERMILK PUDDING

- baked rhubarb with strawberries (see page 146) + whole strawberries
- gooseberry sauce (see page 151) + elderflowers
- cherry sauce (see page 144) + maraschino cherries
- shaken redcurrants (see page 150) + bunches of fresh redcurrants

YELLOW SAGO PUDDING
with COCONUT

When I was a child, my mother sometimes used to make a very filling yellow sago soup with egg yolks, lemon and whole prunes. Although it sounds as if I grew up in the 1950s, I'm actually a child of the 80s, but I guess I was lucky enough to have a mother with a repertoire of old-fashioned desserts. I loved the texture of those potato starch pearls, which we knew as sago, as they rolled over the tongue like little beads of fun, so I was devastated to discover I could no longer find them. The demand for potato starch pearls declined to such an extent that the factory that used to make them stopped their production. I have nevertheless created a pudding with mock sago — perhaps together we can create new demand for the real thing. Until that happens though, I use tapioca pearls bought from an Oriental supermarket as a good substitute. Now that cassava root starch and not potato starch binds the little pearls together, this pudding has also been given an Asian feel with coconut and lime.

Makes 1.5 litres/6 cups, serves 8–10
FOR THE PUDDING MIXTURE
5 leaves gelatine

600 ml/2½ cups whole milk

1 (400-ml/1⅜ cups) tin coconut milk

100 g/4 oz tapioca pearls (or potato
 starch pearls)

4 egg yolks

100 g/½ cup sugar

Zest of 1 organic lime

Juice of 2 small limes

200 ml/⅞ cup whipping cream

Soak the gelatine in a large bowl of cold water.

Combine the milk, coconut milk and tapioca pearls in a heavy-based saucepan. Cook over a low heat for 10–12 minutes to a creamy porridge. Remove from the heat and allow to cool slightly. Take the gelatine out of the water, squeeze out the

excess liquid, and add it to the warm porridge.

Beat the egg yolks with the sugar until fluffy, and then stir in the warm porridge together with the grated lime zest and lime juice. Cool the porridge and egg mixture in the refrigerator, although not for long because it sets quickly.

Beat the whipping cream into soft peaks and fold it into the cool porridge. First fold in a small amount until smooth. Then gently fold in the rest of the soft-whipped cream.

Pour the pudding mixture into a suitable mould that has been rinsed in cold water, and refrigerate until firmly set, for at least 6 hours, or overnight.

See pages 34–37 for instructions on unmoulding the pudding.

Decorate the pudding with whipped cream swirls, coconut and possibly fruits or berries, depending on the occasion.

SUITABLE ACCOMPANIMENTS + DECORATIONS FOR
YELLOW SAGO PUDDING *with* COCONUT

- banana and passion fruit compote (see page 142) + fresh coconut flakes
- chocolate sauce (see pages 150–151) + whipped cream swirls and toasted coconut flakes
- cherry sauce (see page 144) + maraschino cherries
- fresh mango + flakes of fresh coconut

DIPLOMAT PUDDING

Vanilla bavarois layered with candied fruit and macaroons, that's what a diplo-mat pudding is all about. Practically a jellied trifle, it was traditionally packed with currants, raisins, Seville oranges and other delicacies. In my version, however, it is prunes, Armagnac and maraschino cherries that uphold its status. In the old days it would have been served with a fruit juice thickened to a sauce with po-tato starch, or with a crème anglaise, but I prefer it with a little whipped cream. If you want extra accompaniments, cherry sauce or fresh cherries are just the thing.

Makes 1.5 litres/6 cups, serves 8–10

FOR THE BAVAROIS

7 leaves gelatine	8 egg yolks
400 ml/1⅜ cups whole milk	2 tbsp Armagnac
300 ml/1¼ cups whipping cream	300 ml/1¼ cups whipping cream
160 g/¾ cup sugar	(for later addition)
2 vanilla pods	

FOR THE FILLING

150 g/6 oz soft prunes	75 g/3 oz macaroons
50 g/2 oz maraschino cherries	50 ml/3 tbsp Armagnac

Soak the gelatine in a large bowl of cold water.

Combine the milk, first amount of cream and a couple of tablespoons of the sugar in a heavy-based saucepan together with the split vanilla pods and scraped-out seeds. Place over a low heat until just short of boiling. Remove from the heat, cover the pan with a lid, and allow the vanilla to infuse in the milk and cream mixture for 10–15 minutes.

Beat the egg yolks and remaining sugar together in a large bowl.

Heat the vanilla-flavoured milk and cream mixture until just short of boiling. Pour it hot into the egg and sugar mixture while whisking vigorously. Transfer everything

back into the pan and heat gently over a low heat while stirring with a silicone spatula or a wooden spoon until the temperature reaches 83–85ºC (180–185°F). Do NOT allow the mixture to boil. The custard should be neither too runny nor too thick. Ideally, it should have a consistency that coats the back of a spoon (it should stick to the surface of the spatula or spoon without running off).

Immediately remove the pan from the heat. Take the gelatine out of the water and squeeze out the excess liquid. Add it to the warm custard. Stir until the gelatine dissolves. Pour the custard through a sieve into a bowl and add the Armagnac. Allow it to cool slightly and then refrigerate. It should be cold in about 1–2 hours, and it may have set slightly around the edges of the bowl.

Beat the remaining cream into soft peaks. First fold a small amount into the chilled custard until smooth. Then gently fold in the rest of the soft-whipped cream.

Return the bavarois to the refrigerator and allow it to set a little more, otherwise the filling will sink to the bottom of the pudding.

Cut the prunes into bite-sized chunks and remove stems from the maraschino cherries. Crumble the macaroons into a deep dish and drizzle them with Armagnac.

Pour some of the bavarois into a suitable mould that has been rinsed with water. Add a layer of prunes and crumbled macaroons and then another layer of bavarois, and continue layering just like when you are making a trifle. Finish with a layer of bavarois.

Refrigerate until firmly set, for at least 6 hours, or overnight.

See pages 34–37 for instructions on unmoulding the pudding.

Decorate the pudding with prunes and perhaps maraschino cherries.

SUITABLE ACCOMPANIMENTS + DECORATIONS FOR
DIPLOMAT PUDDING

- prunes sprinkled with Armagnac + maraschino cherries
- prunes in Earl Grey syrup (see page 148) + whipped cream swirls
- cherry sauce (see page 144) + maraschino cherries

LEMON PUDDING

If you like lemon mousse, you'll love this pudding. Although less airy and much wobblier than its mousse counterpart, this pudding has a fine balance between tartness, sweetness and richness. When they are in season in February and March, I replace lemons with bergamot oranges to make the most delicious, citrusy, bergamot pudding flavoured with Earl Grey tea, which reminds me of the sweets I used to suck as a child. I serve the pudding with whipped cream or meringue, and with a really good and deliciously tangy salted caramel sauce.

Makes 1.2 litres/5 cups, serves 6–8

FOR THE BAVAROIS

7 leaves gelatine

8 egg yolks

180 g/⅞ cup sugar

400 ml/1⅜ cups whole milk

300 ml/1¼ cups whipping cream

Juice of 3 lemons (for 120 ml/½ cup juice)

Zest of 1 organic lime

300 ml/1¼ cups whipping cream (for later addition)

Soak the gelatine in a large bowl of cold water.

Set aside a couple of tablespoons of sugar and beat the rest together with the egg yolks in a large mixing bowl.

Combine the milk, first amount of cream and reserved sugar in a heavy-based saucepan. Place over a low heat until just short of boiling.

Pour the hot milk and cream mixture into the egg and sugar mixture, whisking vigorously. Transfer everything back into the pan and heat gently over a low heat while stirring with a silicone spatula or a wooden spoon until the temperature reaches 83–85°C (180–185°F). Do NOT allow the mixture to boil. The custard should be neither too runny nor too thick. Ideally, it should have a consistency that coats the back of a spoon (it should stick to the surface of the spatula or spoon without running off).

Immediately remove the pan from the heat. Take the gelatine out of the water and

squeeze out the excess liquid. Add it to the warm custard. Stir until the gelatine dissolves. Pass the custard through a sieve into a bowl. Allow it to cool slightly before
adding the lemon juice and zest and then refrigerate. It should be cold in about 1–2
hours, and it may have set slightly around the edges of the bowl. Stir the custard a
few times while cooling, to prevent the lemon juice from separating.

Beat the remaining cream into soft peaks. First fold a small amount into the chilled
custard until smooth. Then gently fold in the rest of the soft-whipped cream.

Pour the bavarois into a suitable mould that has been rinsed in cold water, and
refrigerate until firmly set, for at least 6 hours, or overnight.

See pages 34–37 for instructions on unmoulding the pudding.

Decorate with swirls of whipped cream or meringue (see tip), and perhaps small
daisies or kumquat slices.

Tip

If you have a chef's blowtorch, you can give the pudding a lemon meringue
pie twist: Beat 2 egg whites at medium speed to soft peaks. Then add 120
g/½ cup of sugar, a spoonful at a time, and continue to beat at medium
speed until all the sugar is used up and the meringue is shiny and stiff. Use a
piping bag to pipe the meringue onto the pudding just before serving, and
colour it a little with the blowtorch. Since it isn't possible to make a smaller
quantity of meringue, use the leftover to make meringue kisses.

SUITABLE ACCOMPANIMENTS + DECORATIONS FOR
LEMON PUDDING

- meringue or whipped cream swirls (see tip) + daisies (see important information on page 33)
- orange salad with orange flower water and cocoa nibs (see page 152) + sliced kumquats
- salted caramel sauce (see page 143)
- prunes in Earl Grey syrup (see page 148) + whipped cream swirls

STRAWBERRY *and* VANILLA PUDDING

A pink pudding that tastes of summer, sunshine and strawberry tartlets. If you want to bring out the flavour of strawberry tartlets filled with pastry cream, serve the pudding with a warm chocolate sauce. If not, then use fresh berries or stewed rhubarb! You can also make a wonderful raspberry pudding using this recipe; in this case, use less lemon juice, since raspberries are already more acidic than strawberries.

Makes 1.7 litres/7 cups, serves 10–12

FOR THE BAVAROIS

7 leaves gelatine

400 ml/1⅜ cups whole milk

300 ml/1¼ cups whipping cream

2 vanilla pods

190 g/scant 1 cup sugar

8 egg yolks

300 ml/1¼ cups whipping cream
  (for later addition)

FOR THE STRAWBERRY PURÉE

400 g/14 oz ripe strawberries

The juice of about ½ a lemon

Soak the gelatine in a large bowl of cold water.

Combine the milk, first amount of cream and a couple of tablespoons of the sugar in a heavy-based saucepan together with the split vanilla pods and scraped-out seeds. Place over a low heat until just short of boiling. Remove from the heat, cover the pan with a lid, and allow the vanilla to infuse in the milk and cream mixture for 10–15 minutes.

Beat the egg yolks and remaining sugar together in a large bowl.

Heat the vanilla-flavoured milk and cream mixture until just short of boiling. Pour it hot into the egg and sugar mixture while whisking vigorously. Transfer everything back into the pan and heat gently over a low heat while stirring with a silicone spatula or a wooden spoon until the temperature reaches 83–85°C (180–185°F). [cont.]

Do NOT allow the mixture to boil. The custard should be neither too runny nor too thick. Ideally, it should have a consistency that coats the back of a spoon (it should stick to the surface of the spatula or spoon without running off).

Immediately remove the pan from the heat. Take the gelatine out of the water and squeeze out the excess liquid. Add it to the warm custard. Stir until the gelatine dissolves. Pass the custard through a sieve into a bowl.

Refrigerate. It should be cold in about 1–2 hours, and it may have set slightly around the edges of the bowl.

Rinse and hull the strawberries, and combine with the lemon juice in a blender. Blend to a smooth purée. Stir the strawberry purée into the custard. Blend a little more with a hand-held blender to make it extra smooth.

Beat the remaining cream into soft peaks. First fold a small amount into the chilled custard until smooth. Then gently fold in the rest of the soft-whipped cream.

Pour the bavarois into a suitable mould that has been rinsed in cold water. Refrigerate until firmly set, for at least 6 hours, or overnight.

See pages 34–37 for instructions on unmoulding the pudding.

Decorate the pudding with whipped cream swirls, fresh strawberries and edible flowers.

SUITABLE ACCOMPANIMENTS + DECORATIONS FOR
STRAWBERRY *and* VANILLA PUDDING

- whipped cream swirls, fresh strawberries + elderflowers
- crème anglaise (see page 147) + fresh strawberries and lemon balm
- baked rhubarb with strawberries (see page 146) + roses
- chocolate sauce (see pages 150–151) + fresh strawberries

SALTED CARAMEL PUDDING

Caramel is delicious on its own, but its sweet, burnt flavour is enhanced with a pinch of sea salt. For a flashy American touch, I top the pudding with the world's best salted caramel sauce and a mound of crunchy caramel popcorn. When I'm not feeling so extravagant, I decorate it with ... ah, who am I trying to fool? Salted caramel pudding always puts me in the mood for extravagance!

Makes 1.2 litres/5 cups, serves 6–8

FOR THE CARAMEL SYRUP

6 leaves gelatine	200 ml/⅞ cup boiling water
½ tsp sea salt	100 g/⅜ cup sugar

FOR THE BAVAROIS

8 egg yolks	200 ml/⅞ cup whipping cream
70 g/⅓ cup brown sugar	250 ml/1 cup whipping cream
300 ml/1¼ cups whole milk	(for later addition)

Soak the gelatine in a large bowl of cold water.

Dissolve the salt in boiling water in a small jug or bowl.

Sprinkle the sugar for the caramel into a dry sauté pan or frying pan and melt it into a bubbling light golden-brown caramel. Remove the pan from the heat and carefully pour in the water. Be very careful, as it will splatter. Cook until any lumps of sugar have dissolved, leaving a runny caramel syrup. Transfer the syrup to a bowl or a measuring jug with a spout, and leave it to cool slightly.

Take the gelatine out of the water, squeeze out the excess liquid, and add it to the warm caramel syrup. Stir until the gelatine is dissolved, then leave to stand.

Now make the bavarois. Set aside a tablespoon of sugar and beat the rest together with the egg yolks in a large mixing bowl.

Combine the milk, the first amount of cream and the reserved sugar in a heavy-

based saucepan. Place over a low heat until just short of boiling.

Pour the hot milk and cream mixture into the egg and sugar mixture, whisking vigorously. Transfer everything back into the pan and heat gently over a low heat while stirring with a silicone spatula until the temperature reaches 83–85°C (180–185°F). Do NOT allow the mixture to boil. The custard should be neither too runny nor too thick. Ideally, it should have a consistency that coats the back of a spoon (it should stick to the surface of the spatula without running off).

Immediately remove the pan from the heat. Whisk the caramel syrup into the custard. Pass the custard through a sieve into a bowl. Allow it to cool slightly and then refrigerate. It should be cold in about 1–2 hours, and it may have set slightly around the edges of the bowl.

Beat the remaining cream into soft peaks. First fold a small amount into the chilled custard until smooth. Then gently fold in the rest of the soft-whipped cream.

Pour the bavarois into a suitable mould that has been rinsed in cold water. Refrigerate until firmly set, for at least 6 hours, or overnight.

See pages 34–37 for instructions on unmoulding the pudding.

Decorate the pudding by pouring salted caramel (see opposite) or chocolate sauce over it, and top with caramel popcorn, or whatever else takes your fancy.

SUITABLE ACCOMPANIMENTS + DECORATIONS FOR
SALT CARAMEL PUDDING

- salted caramel sauce (see page 143) + salted caramel popcorn (see below)
- chocolate sauce (see pages 150–151) + banana and salted peanuts
- salted caramel sauce (see page 143) and banana and passion fruit compote (see page 142)

SALTED CARAMEL POPCORN

60 g/2¼ oz popcorn (popped weight)

90 g/6 tbsp butter

110 g/½ cup brown sugar

½ tsp sea salt

¼ tsp baking powder

Start by popping the popcorn according to the instructions on the packet, or buy a bag of good ready-popped popcorn.

Preheat the oven to 120°C (250°F, gas ½).

Combine the butter, sugar and salt in a large, heavy-based saucepan, and cook until the sugar melts into the butter and the mixture bubbles. Add the baking powder, and then quickly stir the popped popcorn into the caramel until well and evenly coated. Spread the popcorn out over a baking tray lined with baking parchment, and bake in the warm oven for about 45 minutes until dry and crispy.

Take the popcorn out of the oven, leave to cool and store in an airtight container until ready to use.

REDCURRANT PUDDING

Like citrus fruits, redcurrants provide plenty of aromatic tartness, a welcome addition to desserts made with custard and large amounts of cream. That's why I had to make this pudding. Actually, I would have preferred to have made it as an old fashioned bavarois made with fruit juice, a good redcurrant juice in this case. However, it's almost impossible to find a decent redcurrant juice unless you make it yourself. Nevertheless, it is at least as good and much easier to make with the fresh, tangy berries. If you would like to give even more flavour to the pudding, you can heat the milk and cream mixture with some vanilla, geranium leaves or lemon verbena, and leave it to infuse for a while before heating it back up to make the bavarois.

Makes 1.2 litres/5 cups, serves 6–8

FOR THE BAVAROIS

7 leaves gelatine

8 egg yolks

180 g/⅞ cup sugar

400 ml/1⅜ cups whole milk

300 ml/1¼ cups whipping cream

300 g/10 oz redcurrants

Juice of ½ lemon

300 ml/1¼ cups whipping cream
  (for later addition)

Soak the gelatine in a large bowl of cold water.

Set aside a couple of tablespoons of sugar and beat the rest together with the egg yolks in a large mixing bowl.

Combine the milk, first amount of cream and reserved sugar in a heavy-based saucepan. Place over a low heat until just short of boiling.

Pour the hot milk and cream mixture into the egg and sugar mixture, whisking vigorously. Transfer everything back into the pan and heat gently over a low heat while stirring with a silicone spatula or a wooden spoon until the temperature reaches 83–85°C [180–185°F]. Do NOT allow the mixture to boil. The custard should be neither too runny nor too thick. Ideally, it should have a consistency that coats

the back of a spoon (it should stick to the surface of the spatula or spoon without running off).

Immediately remove the pan from the heat. Take the gelatine out of the water and squeeze out the excess liquid. Add it to the warm custard. Stir until the gelatine dissolves. Pass the custard through a sieve into a bowl and allow it to cool slightly. Meanwhile, put the redcurrants into a blender with the lemon juice. Blend to a purée and then pass through a sieve. Use the back of a spoon to push all of the juice and purée through the sieve. Stir the redcurrant purée into the custard and refrigerate. It should be cold in about 1–2 hours, and it may have set slightly around the edges of the bowl.

Beat the remaining cream into soft peaks. First fold a small amount into the chilled custard until smooth. Then gently fold in the rest of the soft-whipped cream.

Pour the bavarois into a suitable mould that has been rinsed in cold water, and refrigerate until firmly set, for at least 6 hours, or overnight.

See pages 34–37 for instructions on unmoulding the pudding.

Decorate with whipped cream swirls, bunches of fresh redcurrants, redcurrant jelly or whatever comes to mind.

SUITABLE ACCOMPANIMENTS + DECORATIONS FOR
REDCURRANT PUDDING

- meringue (see tip page 102) + fresh redcurrants
- whipped cream swirls + redcurrant jelly
- salted caramel sauce (see page 143) + fresh redcurrants
- crème anglaise (see page 147) + shaken redcurrants (see page 150)

LAYERED VANILLA *and* CHERRY PUDDING

Custard and cherries make a great flavour combination. A classic almond or vanilla bavarois with cherry sauce is one of the best desserts you can make, and if you join the two things together, it goes without saying that the result will be excellent. Who wouldn't be thrilled with a red and white striped birthday pudding with cherry jelly and vanilla custard? Choose a large and deep mould, so that the layers of the pudding will stand out in all their glory. The pudding isn't difficult to make, but just a word of warning: it is time-consuming, since it must be set one layer at a time. You also have to be careful when unmoulding, because the bavarois and the jelly have to be released from the sides of the mould at the same time (helped by dipping the mould in warm water and the entry of air – see pages 35–36), before you shake it; otherwise, you risk having the pudding coming apart in layers.

Makes 1.7 litres/7 cups, serves 10–12

FOR THE CHERRY JELLY

7 leaves gelatine
600 ml/2½ cups good-quality raw cherry juice (or juice from preserved cherries)

FOR THE VANILLA BAVAROIS

7 leaves gelatine
300 ml/1¼ cups whipping cream
400 ml/1⅜ cups whole milk
160 g/¾ cup sugar

2 vanilla pods
8 egg yolks
300 ml/1¼ cups whipping cream (for
  later addition)

Start by soaking 2 of the 7 gelatine leaves in a bowl of cold water.
Heat 200 ml/⅞ cup of cherry juice in a small saucepan and stir in the soaked gelatine to dissolve. Pour the jelly mixture into the bottom of a large pudding mould, and refrigerate for 1–2 hours until the jelly is soft set.
[cont.]

Soak the gelatine for the bavarois in a large bowl of cold water.

Combine the first amount of cream with the milk and a couple of tablespoons of the sugar in a heavy-based saucepan together with the split vanilla pod and scraped-out seeds. Place over a low heat and heat until just short of boiling. Remove from the heat, cover the pan with a lid, and allow the vanilla to infuse in the milk and cream mixture for 10–15 minutes.

Beat the egg yolks and remaining sugar together in a large bowl.

Heat the vanilla-flavoured milk and cream mixture until just short of boiling. Then pour the hot mixture into the egg and sugar mixture while whisking vigorously. Transfer everything back into the pan and heat gently over a low heat while stirring with a silicone spatula or a wooden spoon until the temperature reaches 83–85°C (180–185°F). Do NOT allow the mixture to boil. The custard should be neither too runny nor too thick. Ideally, it should have a consistency that coats the back of a spoon (it should stick to the surface of the spatula or spoon without running off).

Immediately remove the pan from the heat. Take the gelatine out of the water and squeeze out the excess liquid. Add it to the warm custard. Stir until the gelatine dissolves. Pass the custard through a sieve into a bowl. Allow it to cool slightly and then refrigerate. It should be cold in about 1–2 hours, and it may have set slightly around the edges of the bowl.

Beat the remaining cream into soft peaks. First fold a small amount into the chilled custard until smooth. Then gently fold in the rest of the soft-whipped cream.

Pour the bavarois into the mould over the soft cherry jelly, and refrigerate until it is almost fully set. This should take about 3-4 hours.

Now soak the remaining 5 leaves of gelatine for the jelly in a bowl of cold water.

Heat half of the 400 ml/1³/₈ cups of cherry juice in a small saucepan, and stir in the soaked gelatine until it dissolves. Pour the jelly mixture into a bowl, and combine with the remaining cherry juice. Allow the juice to cool and begin to set quite a bit around the edges of the bowl, and then pour it over the set bavarois. Refrigerate for 4-6 hours or overnight.

See pages 34–37 for instructions on unmoulding the pudding.

Decorate the pudding with flags or cherries, or with decorations to suit the occasion.

SUITABLE ACCOMPANIMENTS + DECORATIONS FOR
LAYERED VANILLA *and* CHERRY PUDDING

- crème anglaise (see page 147) + preserved cherries
- cherry sauce with amaretto (see page 144) + maraschino cherries
- whipped cream swirls and paper flags
- fresh cherry + baby's breath (see important information on page 33)

Tip

If you use preserved cherries for the juice, you can add some of the cherries to the jelly if you like. Let the jelly set a little around the edges of the mould before inserting the cherries.

BLACKBERRY PUDDING

I grew up on a small farm where wild blackberry bushes grew along the stone wall separating my parents' land from that of our neighbours. It was an autumn tradition for the entire family to clamber over the wall and pick large amounts of berries for jam and for my mother's blackberry tart consisting of a shortcrust pastry case filled with blackberry mousse and garnished with whole blackberries. There is a straight line connecting the best flavours from my childhood with those that I pursue as an adult, so now you know why I absolutely had to feature a blackberry pudding in this book.

Makes 1.7 litres/7 cups, serves 10–12

FOR THE BAVAROIS

400 g/14 oz frozen or fresh blackberries

Juice of 1 lemon

8 leaves gelatine

400 ml/1⅜ cups whole milk

300 ml/1¼ cups whipping cream

190 g/scant 1 cup sugar

2 vanilla pods

8 egg yolks

300 ml/1¼ cups whipping cream (for later addition)

If you are using frozen berries, leave them to thaw out in a saucepan before giving them a quick boil. If using fresh blackberries, just rinse them. Combine the fresh/boiled blackberries with the lemon juice in a blender. Briefly blend, and then pass the mixture through a sieve into a bowl. Use the back of a spoon to push all of juice and pulp through the sieve to obtain a purée.

Soak the gelatine in a large bowl of cold water.

Combine the milk, first amount of cream and a couple of tablespoons of the sugar in a heavy-based saucepan together with the split vanilla pods and scraped-out seeds. Place over a low heat until just short of boiling. Remove from the heat, cover the pan with a lid, and allow the vanilla to infuse in the milk and cream mixture for 10–15 minutes.

[cont.]

Beat the egg yolks and remaining sugar together in a large bowl.

Heat the vanilla-flavoured milk and cream mixture until just short of boiling. Pour it hot into the egg and sugar mixture while whisking vigorously. Transfer everything back into the pan and heat gently over a low heat while stirring with a silicone spatula or a wooden spoon until the temperature reaches 83–85°C (180–185°F). Do NOT allow the mixture to boil. The custard should be neither too runny nor too thick. Ideally, it should have a consistency that coats the back of a spoon (it should stick to the surface of the spatula or spoon without running off).

Immediately remove the pan from the heat. Take the gelatine out of the water, squeeze out the excess liquid, and add it to the warm custard. Stir until the gelatine dissolves. Pass the custard through a sieve into a bowl.

Stir in the sieved blackberry purée into the custard. Blend lightly if necessary with a hand-held blender to make it extra smooth. Refrigerate. It should be cold in about 1–2 hours, and it may have set slightly around the edges of the bowl.

Beat the remaining cream into soft peaks. First fold a small amount into the chilled custard until smooth. Then gently fold in the rest of the soft-whipped cream.

Pour the bavarois into a suitable mould that has been rinsed in cold water. Refrigerate until firmly set, for at least 6 hours, or overnight.

See pages 34–37 for instructions on unmoulding the pudding.

Decorate the pudding with fresh blackberries and blackberry leaves or red sorrel.

SUITABLE ACCOMPANIMENTS + DECORATIONS FOR
BLACKBERRY PUDDING

- fresh blackberries + blackberry leaves and whipped cream swirls
- blackberry sauce (see page 153) + fresh blackberries and red sorrel
- baked apricots with pistachios (see page 145) + whipped cream swirls

RED JELLY RING

There are bavarois puddings served with a fruit sauce, and then there are jelly rings served with crème anglaise. I refer to the latter as 'inverted puddings'. These are hardly ever served nowadays, even though many people love them, especially children. The way they wobble and then burst in your mouth is a delight, and there is nothing quite like squeezing a mouthful of jelly through your front teeth, or so they say. My father tells the story of how, for his confirmation, all he ordered was a red jelly ring with crème anglaise. So this one is dedicated to you, dad. I use a good juice that I buy, but feel free to make your own.

Makes 1.5 litres/6 cups, serves 8–10

FOR THE JELLY MIXTURE

8 leaves gelatine

500 ml/2 cups quality undiluted
   raspberry juice

300 ml/1¼ cups water

700 g/1½ lbs mixed red fruits
   (raspberries, strawberries, redcurrants
   and cherries)

Soak the gelatine in a large bowl of cold water for about 10 minutes.

Warm about 200 ml/⅞ cup of the juice in a saucepan, stirring constantly. Take the gelatine out of the water, squeeze out the excess liquid, and add it to the juice. Stir until the gelatine dissolves. Add the rest of the juice and water, and mix well.

Rinse and hull the fruit, then pat dry with paper towels. If using strawberries, slice if necessary, and if using cherries, pit first.

Evenly arrange half of the fruit in a savarin mould or pudding mould, and pour in about half of the jelly mixture to cover. Carefully place the mould in the refrigerator and allow the jelly to set. This should take about 1–2 hours. Set aside the rest of the jelly mixture.

Take the mould out of the refrigerator, and arrange the rest of the fruit evenly over the top of the jelly. Cover them with the remaining jelly mixture and carefully return

the mould to the refrigerator and allow the jelly to set, for 4–6 hours or overnight. Unmould the jelly in the same way as you would a pudding (see pages 34–37).

The glossy red jelly is beautiful on its own, but you can decorate it with fresh elder-flowers, lemon balm, geranium or mint.
Serve with crème anglaise or raw cream for an 'inverted pudding' effect.

SUITABLE ACCOMPANIMENTS + DECORATIONS FOR
RED JELLY RING

- crème anglaise (see page 147) + pink roses, carnations or peonies (see important information on page 33)
- raw cream (see page 154) + geranium, mint or lemon balm
- whipped cream + elderflowers

RAW RHUBARB JELLY

It may not seem like anything special, but I promise you that this pink dessert tastes wonderful. My grandmother used to make 'raw' rhubarb juice with the same extraction method used to make elderflower cordial. It is this juice that I have transformed here into a wobbly dessert. The juice should be left to infuse the day before it is going to be sieved and jellied. Doing it this way will give a much tastier result than using a boiled or bought juice. Rhubarb can vary, so taste the juice. It may need a little more sugar, and you might need to dilute it with a little water before you turn it into jelly.

Makes 1–1.5 litres/4-5 cups, serves 6–10

FOR THE JELLY MIXTURE

1 kg/2 lbs rhubarb

20 g/2 tbsp cream of tartar

900 ml/3¾ cups boiling water

300 g/1½ cups sugar (or more if you prefer a sweeter juice)

10–15 leaves gelatine (1 leaf per 100 ml/⅜ cup of juice)

Clean the rhubarb and slice finely. Place in a large bowl with the cream of tartar. Pour the boiling water over the rhubarb. Allow it to cool to room temperature before covering the bowl with cling film and putting in the refrigerator. Leave the rhubarb to infuse for 1 day.

Pass the juice through a very fine sieve and discard the rhubarb. Stir the sugar into the cold juice. Taste the juice; you may need to use more sugar than the amount given.

Measure out the juice to determine how many sheets of gelatine to use – allow 1 sheet per 100 ml/⅜ cup of juice.

Soak the gelatine in a large bowl of cold water for about 10 minutes.

Warm about 200 ml/⅞ cup of the juice in a saucepan, stirring constantly. Take the gelatine out of the water, squeeze out the excess liquid, and add it to the juice. Stir until the gelatine dissolves. Add the rest of the juice and stir in the pan so that they are thoroughly dissolved. Pour the rhubarb juice into a savarin mould or pudding

mould, then refrigerate and allow the jelly to set, for 4–6 hours or overnight. Unmould the jelly in the same way as you would a pudding (see pages 34–37).

Serve this lovely jelly with sugared strawberries and cold crème anglaise.

Tip

If you would like to flavour the rhubarb jelly, add 3 rose geranium leaves or a small handful of sweet woodruff together with the cream of tartar when you make the juice.

SUITABLE ACCOMPANIMENTS + DECORATIONS FOR
RAW RHUBARB JELLY

- crème anglaise (see page 147) + sugared strawberries
- raw cream (see page 154) + fresh strawberries and roses
- baked rhubarb with strawberries (see page 146) + whipped cream swirls

MIDSUMMER JELLY *with* ELDERFLOWER & STRAWBERRIES

At midsummer, when the elder trees are blooming and the first strawberries are ripe and ready to be picked, this jelly makes a lovely, easy dessert. On the other hand, it can only be as good as the elderflower cordial you use, and works best of all with the home-made version. Since cordials can vary, it may be necessary to adjust the amount of water and lemon juice. If you end up with a different quantity of liquid than described, remember to allow for 1 leaf of gelatine per 100 ml/⅜ cup of liquid.

Makes 1.5 litres/5 cups, serves 8–10

FOR THE JELLY MIXTURE

8 leaves gelatine

500 ml/2 cups quality undiluted
   elderflower cordial

250 ml/1 cup water

Juice of 1 lemon

700 g/1½ lbs strawberries

Soak the gelatine in a large bowl of cold water for about 10 minutes.

Warm about 200 ml/⅞ cup of elderflower cordial in a saucepan, stirring constantly. Take the gelatine out of the water, squeeze out the excess liquid, and add it to the cordial. Stir until the gelatine dissolves. Add the rest of the cordial and water and mix well. Squeeze the lemon and add the juice to the elderflower mixture.

Rinse and hull the strawberries, then pat dry with paper towels. Evenly arrange half of the strawberries in a savarin mould or pudding mould, and pour in about half of the jelly mixture to cover. Carefully place the mould in the refrigerator and allow the jelly to set. This should take about 1–2 hours. Set aside the rest of the jelly mixture.

Take the mould out of the refrigerator, and arrange the rest of the strawberries evenly over the top of the jelly. Cover them with the remaining jelly mixture and carefully return the mould to the refrigerator and allow the jelly to set, for 4–6 hours or overnight.

[cont.]

Unmould the jelly in the same way as you would a pudding (see pages 34–37).

Serve with crème anglaise or raw cream for an 'inverted pudding' effect.

SUITABLE ACCOMPANIMENTS + DECORATIONS FOR
MIDSUMMER JELLY *with* ELDERFLOWER & STRAWBERRY

- crème anglaise (see page 147) + small strawberries
- raw cream (see page 154) + fresh elderflowers

GRAPEFRUIT JELLY *with* CONDENSED MILK & CARDAMOM

An 'inverted pudding' is not only lovely in summer, when there are lots of berries to be had. It also good in winter as a light dessert that wobbles nicely on its dish. This time is consists of fresh pink grapefruit jelly, which rests on a layer of sweet, cardamom-infused condensed milk jelly. You can serve this jelly dessert as it is, or add a creamy element with a warm crème anglaise, to which you can also easily add a few cardamom pods, together with the vanilla. Or simply leave out the milk jelly layer and instead make a double portion of the stunning pink grapefruit jelly!

Makes 1.2 litres/4 cups, serves 6–8

FOR THE GRAPEFRUIT JELLY

9 leaves gelatine
500 ml/2 cups fresh grapefruit juice (from about 4 pink grapefruit)
110 g/½ cup sugar

FOR THE MILK JELLY

6 leaves gelatine
1 (397-g /14 oz) tin condensed milk

400 ml/1⅜ cups whole milk
15 green cardamom pods

Soak the gelatine for the grapefruit jelly in a large bowl of cold water for about 10 minutes.

Squeeze the grapefruits, which should yield about 500 ml/2 cups. If there is too little, you can make up for the shortfall with a little water.

Heat about 200 ml/⅞ cup of the grapefruit juice up together with the sugar until it dissolves. Take the gelatine out of the water, squeeze out the excess liquid, and add it to the juice. Stir until the gelatine dissolves. Pour the cold grapefruit juice into the hot juice and stir the mixture thoroughly.

[cont.]

Pour the grapefruit jelly mixture into the bottom of a suitable mould and refrigerate until the jelly is soft set. It should take 2–3 hours.

Now make the milk jelly. Soak the gelatine in a large bowl of cold water. Mix the condensed milk and the whole milk in a small saucepan and add the cardamom pods. Bring to the boil over a low heat, stirring to prevent the condensed milk from burning. Remove from the heat and allow the cardamom to infuse for 10 minutes. Warm the milk up again slightly. Drain the excess water from the gelatine and add to the milk. Pass the mixture through a sieve over a bowl and set aside to cool somewhat before placing it in the refrigerator. Allow it to cool enough so that it begins to set against the sides of the bowl.

Spoon the mixture over the grapefruit jelly and return the mould to the refrigerator for 4–6 hours, or overnight.
Unmould the jelly in the same way as you would a pudding (see pages 34–37).

Serve on its own or with crème anglaise and perhaps a fresh orange or grapefruit salad.

SUITABLE ACCOMPANIMENTS + DECORATIONS FOR
GRAPEFRUIT JELLY *with* CONDENSED MILK & CARDAMOM

- crème anglaise (see page 147) + cardamom pods
- orange salad with orange flower water and cocoa nibs (see page 152) + whipped cream swirls
- grapefruit salad (similar to the orange salad, see page 152) + white roses, carnations or peonies (see important information on page 33)

PUDDING ACCOMPANIMENTS

BANANA AND PASSION FRUIT COMPOTE

Sometimes you need a sharp taste to cut through the rich creaminess of a bavarois. On such occasions, I serve banana and passion fruit compote, whose tropical flavour particularly suits chocolate pudding, rum pudding and, of course, sago pudding with coconut. It is very important to use ripe bananas. Unripe bananas leave a nasty astringent taste in the mouth when warmed. Brown spots are welcome.

Makes about 400 ml/1⅜ cups, serves 6–8

4 passion fruit

3 ripe bananas

Juice of 1 orange

75 g/¼ cup + 2 tbsp sugar

Scoop out the flesh from the passion fruit into a small saucepan. Mash one banana on a plate and add to the saucepan with the passion fruit, together with the orange juice and sugar. Simmer the compote for 5 minutes.

Cut the last two bananas into small cubes and add them to the compote. Simmer everything for a few minutes. Taste the compote; you may need to use more sugar than the amount given.

That's all there is to it! Allow the compote to cool before serving.

SALTED CARAMEL SAUCE

Salted caramel sauce has become a kind of signature sauce for many of my puddings. Loved by children and adults alike, it works well with both the heavier chocolate and caramel puddings and with the lighter fruit and classic vanilla bavarois. What's more, it is easy to make. I bought a small, soft plastic bottle which is good for both storing and dispensing the sauce. Salted caramel sauce keeps well in the refrigerator and lends itself equally well to puddings as it does to ice cream, banana hot dogs (banana with caramel sauce, chocolate sauce and cocoa nibs), pancakes and everything else.

Makes about 400 ml/1⅜ cups, serves 8–10
250 g/1¼ cups sugar
25 g/2 tbsp butter
300 ml/1¼ cups whipping cream
½ tsp sea salt

Melt half of the sugar in a heavy-based saucepan to a golden caramel. Add the butter and stir it in. Be very careful, as it will splatter. Stir in the cream a little at a time. A few lumps of caramel may form, but they will dissolve with cooking. Pour in the remaining sugar and cook the sauce through until the sugar and any lumps of caramel have dissolved.
If the sauce seems too thick, add a little more cream.
Add sea salt to taste (be careful not to burn your tongue, it will be very hot!) and allow the caramel to cool to room temperature before serving. Store the caramel sauce in the refrigerator, where it can be kept for up to a week.

CHERRY SAUCE

I love this cherry sauce. The cherries are cooked in amaretto, which acts as a killer almond essence and enhances the wonderful intrinsic almond flavour of the cherries. Yes. You read that right – I cook with amaretto! But it isn't the alcohol that I want in the sauce, merely the flavour. This cherry sauce is relatively thin, so if you prefer a thicker sauce, add a little extra cornflour.

Makes about 800 ml/3⅓ cups, serves 10–12
500 g/1 lb 2 oz pitted cherries, fresh or frozen
125 g/⅔ cup sugar
1 vanilla pod
100 ml/⅜ cup amaretto
100 ml/⅜ cup water
2 tbsp cornflour

Combine the cherries, sugar, split vanilla pod and scraped-out seeds, amaretto and water in a saucepan. If using frozen cherries, put them into the saucepan together with the sugar, and leave them to release their juice and this is absorbed by the sugar, before adding the other ingredients, except the cornflour.
Bring the mixture to the boil, and then gently simmer the cherries for 10–15 minutes. Dissolve the cornflour in a little cold water, and then stir in with the cherries. Continue stirring until the sauce thickens. Cook through for a few minutes.
Allow the sauce to cool before serving.

SHAKEN RASPBERRIES WITH ROSE WATER

Raspberries work well with pudding, however you use them, since they are both acidic and pungent enough to cut through the creaminess of a bavarois. Here, the fresh berries are shaken with sugar and rose water for an easy 'raw' compote.

Serves 4–6
500 g/1 lb 2 oz fresh raspberries
50–75 g/¼ cup + 2 tbsp sugar
2 tbsp rose water

Rinse the raspberries and place them briefly on paper towels to soak up some of the water.

Transfer to a bowl, add the sugar and rose water, and shake gently. Allow the berries to macerate in their juice and serve on the same day.

BAKED APRICOTS WITH PISTACHIOS

When fragrant, rosy French apricots appear at the greengrocer's, I simply can't help myself. Few things say summer as well as fragrant, ripe apricots. All they need is a little time in the oven with some sugar, and there you have it: a fantastic accompaniment for a pudding. A little amaretto won't do any harm; if you don't have any at home, perhaps you should think about getting some in. In the meantime, you can drizzle a little orange juice over the apricots instead.

Serves 6–8
300 g/10 oz (about 10) ripe apricots
50 g/¼ cup sugar
3–4 tbsp amaretto (optional)
3 tbsp unsalted pistachios, shelled

Preheat the oven to 200°C (400°F, gas 6). Cut open the apricots and remove the stone. Place the apricots with the rounded side facing downwards in an ovenproof dish and sprinkle with sugar. Drizzle with amaretto and bake for about 25 minutes until the apricots are tender.

Sprinkle the pistachios over the baked apricots and serve warm or at room temperature.

BAKED RHUBARB WITH STRAWBERRIES

When you bake rhubarb instead of boiling it, you get tender whole pieces of rhubarb in a delicate pink syrup instead of a shredded compote (which is also nice). Once cooled, this rhubarb syrup can be used as a marinade for strawberries, either on their own, or together with the rhubarb pieces, as here. Instead of vanilla, you can add 3–4 geranium leaves to the rhubarb before baking. This adds an exquisite flavour.

Makes 600–700 ml/2½-3 cups, serves 8–10
350 g/12 oz rhubarb (cleaned weight)
80 g/scant ½ cup sugar
1 vanilla pod or 3–4 geranium leaves
250 g/9 oz strawberries

Preheat the oven to 200°C (400°F, gas 6). Cut the rhubarb into small pieces and put them in an ovenproof dish. Set aside 1 teaspoon of the sugar and sprinkle with the rest. Split the vanilla pod, scrape out the seeds and mash them together with the reserved sugar using the flat of a knife to separate the grains. Add the vanilla seed and sugar mixture and the vanilla pod to the dish with the rhubarb and stir.
Bake for about 15 minutes. Gently turn the rhubarb over once while baking. Take the dish out of the oven and let the liquid in the dish cool to room temperature.
Wash and slice the strawberries. Add the strawberries to the rhubarb and syrup. Allow the strawberries to marinate for 1 hour at room temperature before serving.

CRÈME ANGLAISE

The name alone sounds good and old-fashioned... When I make this classic of French cuisine, crème anglaise, the light custard is the base for almost all of the puddings in this book. So, if you've tried making any of them, then you'll be well trained in making crème anglaise. The sauce can be served warm or cold and is the best accompaniment for fruit jellies.

Makes about 500 ml/2 cups, serves 6–8
150 ml whipping cream
200 ml/⅞ cup whole milk
80 g/scant ½ cup sugar
1 vanilla pod
4 egg yolks

Combine the cream with the milk and a couple of tablespoons of the sugar in a heavy-based saucepan together with the split vanilla pod and scraped-out seeds. Place over a low heat and heat until just short of boiling. Remove from the heat, cover the pan with a lid, and allow the vanilla to infuse in the milk and cream mixture for 15 minutes.

Beat the egg yolks and remaining sugar together in a large bowl.

Heat the vanilla-flavoured milk and cream mixture until just short of boiling. Pour it hot into the egg and sugar mixture while whisking vigorously. Transfer everything back into the pan and heat gently over a low heat while stirring with a silicone spatula or a wooden spoon until the temperature reaches 83–85°C (180–185°F). Do NOT allow the mixture to boil. The custard should be neither too runny nor too thick. Ideally, it should have a consistency that coats the back of a spoon (it should stick to the surface of the spatula or spoon without running off).

Immediately pass the sauce through a sieve and into a bowl, cover the surface with cling film, and refrigerate.

Serve the crème anglaise warm or cold.

PRUNES IN EARL GREY SYRUP

The distinctive bergamot taste of these prunes in Early Grey tea syrup goes very well with pudding. These prunes, which have been soaked in tea and coated in prune syrup, go particularly well with vanilla bavarois, diplomat pudding, almond pudding and lemon pudding. They are very sweet, so only serve a few prunes per person.

Serves 6–8
500 ml/2 cups water
15 g/½ oz Earl Grey tea (loose leaf)
300 g/10 oz prunes
1 vanilla pod
Juice of 1 lemon
1 strip organic lemon zest
1 strip organic orange zest
75 g/¼ cup + 2 tbsp sugar

Brew some strong tea using 500 ml/2 cups of boiling water and 15 g/½ oz of Earl Grey tea. Allow the leaves to infuse until the tea is lukewarm. Pour the tea, through a strainer, over the prunes and let them soak for 1½ hours.

Combine the prunes and tea in a heavy-based saucepan with the split vanilla pod and scraped-out vanilla seeds, lemon juice, lemon and orange zest and sugar, and simmer for 15–20 minutes.

Remove the prunes with a slotted spoon, reduce the liquid to a thin syrup. Return the prunes to the syrup and serve them at room temperature.

APPLE COMPOTE

This is an absolutely classic apple compote, which goes well with pudding, apple pie, apple trifle or just with milk. I always make this compote using my favourite apples, either just one variety or a combination of the two. They are very tart and fragrant. But use whichever varieties you prefer.

Makes 500–600 ml/2–2½ cups, serves 6–8
1 kg/2 lbs apples
50 ml/3 tbsp water
1 vanilla pod
75–125 g/⅓–⅔ cup sugar

Peel and core the apples. Coarsely chop and put the pieces in a heavy-based saucepan with the water. Split the vanilla pod, scrape out the seeds and mash them together with a little sugar using the flat of a knife to separate the seeds. Add the vanilla pod and the sugar and seed mixture to the pan Cover the pan with a lid and steam the apples until completely tender – add a little more water along the way if necessary.

Add sugar to the compote (depending on the flavour and tartness of the apples), and beat with a whisk until smooth. Serve warm or cool.

SHAKEN REDCURRANTS

This is the easiest accompaniment for cream desserts. Rinse, hull, shake, mash and serve! Shaken redcurrants are wonderful with any classic bavarois – vanilla, almond, buttermilk and rum (the last without the apple base), while the white chocolate and jasmine tea pudding also suits the tart berries.

Serves 6–8
500 g/1 lb 2 oz fresh redcurrants
200 g/1 cup sugar

Rinse and hull the redcurrants. Combine with the sugar in a bowl together, and mash them up a little with the back of a spoon so that some of them burst. Stir them until the sugar dissolves, and allow them to macerate a little before serving.
Use up the redcurrants on the same day.

CHOCOLATE SAUCE

This chocolate sauce uses chocolate from the French company Valrhona, and has a deliciously thick consistency and a touch of caramel owing to its syrup content. If you don't want the sauce to have a syrupy taste, you can always make a simple sauce using chocolate and plain cream instead.

Makes about 600 ml/2½ cups, serves 6–12
250 g/9 oz dark chocolate, such as Valrhona Caraïbe (66% cocoa) or Manjari
   (64% cocoa)
200 ml/⅞ cup whole milk
100 ml/⅜ cup whipping cream
80 g light syrup (about 6 tablespoons)

Finely chop the chocolate and place in a heatproof bowl. Combine the milk, cream and syrup in a small, heavy-based saucepan, bring to the boil, and pour it slowly into the middle of the chocolate. Allow the chocolate and the warm milk mixture to stand and mingle for about 30 seconds. Stir the mixture with a silicone spatula or wooden spoon so that the chocolate melts outwards from the centre. Give the chocolate sauce a final blitz with a hand-held blender.

Serve the chocolate sauce warm.

If you have trouble getting all the chocolate to melt into the milk and cream mixture, you can always warm the mixture gently in a saucepan or over a bain-marie while stirring.

GOOSEBERRY SAUCE

Ah, gooseberries! These small, hairy berries have an almost exotic taste and make an utterly amazing sauce for puddings. In this version, they are simply cooked with sugar, water and vanilla, but you can also boil the berries until tender in undiluted elderflower cordial.

Makes about 700 ml/3 cups, serves 8–12

500 g/1 lb 2 oz gooseberries

100 g/½ cup sugar

1 vanilla pod

150 ml/⅔ cup water

2 tbsp cornflour (optional)

Rinse the berries, and combine them in a saucepan with the sugar, split vanilla pod, scraped-out vanilla seeds and water. Gently cook the gooseberries for about 15 minutes, until some of them burst.

Taste the sauce and add sugar if necessary as it may not be sweet enough. For a thicker sauce, dissolve the cornflour in a little cold water and stir the mixture into the sauce. Cook through for a few minutes.

Allow the sauce to cool before serving.

ORANGE SALAD WITH ORANGE FLOWER WATER AND COCOA NIBS

Sometimes you need something fresh to contrast with all the creaminess, so try this delicious and easy orange salad. Fruit salads are lovely with cocoa and chocolate puddings, and can also be served with the almond pudding, vanilla bavarois and lemon pudding. If you have any left over, it also tastes good on its own with a dollop of whipped cream.

Serves 6–8
6 oranges
30 g/2 tbsp sugar
3 tbsp orange flower water
3 tbsp cocoa nibs

Peel the oranges with a sharp knife, cutting away all the skin and pith. Slice the oranges across their width into wheels. and arrange them nicely on a large dish. Sprinkle with the sugar and orange flower water and leave to soak into the oranges a little before serving.
Sprinkle the cocoa nibs over the top immediately before serving.

Tip
Cocoa nibs are small pieces of roasted cocoa bean.

BLACKBERRY SAUCE

This is a very simple berry sauce, flavoured with just a little lemon, so as not to overpower the blackberries. If you want to add a kick, you can throw in a couple of whole star anise with the berries as they cook. The sauce can also be made with raspberries. Just leave out the lemon juice.

Makes about 700 ml/3 cups, serves 8–12
500 g/1 lb 2 oz blackberries
100-125g/½ cup sugar
Juice of 1 lemon
50 ml/3 tbsp water
1½–2 tbsp cornflour (optional)

Rinse the berries and combine with the sugar in a saucepan. Don't put in all the sugar; set some aside to adjust the taste. Add the lemon juice and water, and then simmer the berries for 5–10 minutes.

Taste and add more sugar if necessary. The sauce can be thickened with cornflour dissolved in a little cold water. In this case, you should let it cook through for another 2 minutes.

Serve the blackberry sauce warm or cold.

RAW CREAM

Raw cream [literally 'raw custard'] is so old-fashioned and goes so well with fruit desserts, especially fruit jellies. A portion of wobbly raspberry or rhubarb jelly with raw cream is an elegant dessert that is all too rarely served nowadays. This recipe makes enough for 8–10 people, so it suits the jelly dishes or 'inverted puddings'"found in this book.

Makes about 600 ml/2½ cups, serves 6–8
6 egg yolks
130 g/⅔ cup sugar
1 vanilla pod
500 ml/2 cups whipping cream

Beat the egg yolks with the sugar and scraped-out vanilla seeds until thick and pale.
In another bowl, whip the cream until stiff and fold into the egg mixture.
Serve the raw cream on the same day.

STEWED BLACKCURRANTS WITH RUM

Blackcurrants are an acquired taste. They're probably too strong for children, but adults love them. For this reason, some water should be added when making this sauce, as well as a good splash of rum! I like to add the rum for the dark, caramelised flavour that it adds to the clean blackcurrant taste, and not for the alcohol, which is why I let it boil as I make the sauce. But if you do want to give your sauce a boozy edge, add the rum to taste after cooking.

Makes about 900 ml/3¾ cups, serves 10–12
500 g/1 lb 2 oz blackcurrants
250 g/1¼ cups sugar
200 ml/⅞ cup water

25–50 ml/ 2–3 tbsp dark rum

Rinse and hull the blackcurrants and combine in a saucepan with the sugar, water and rum. Simmer for 15–25 minutes until some of the blackcurrants burst and the consistency is thick, similar to a compote. This sauce will thicken as it cools.
Serve cold, warm or at room temperature.

RED JUICE SAUCE

Any old, self-respecting cookbook containing pudding recipes would include red juice sauce as an accompaniment for wobbly bavarois desserts. And this red sauce IS still delicious and loved by children. It can be made from any kind of red juice, but it must be good and tart. I use bought juice when I'm out of home-made juice.

Makes 400–500 ml/1⅜–2 cups, serves 4–6
½ tbsp potato starch
200–300 ml/1¼ cups water
200 ml/⅞ cup undiluted redcurrant or raspberry juice

Mix the potato starch with a little of the water in a small bowl until it thickens.
Pour the juice and the rest of the water into a saucepan. Taste it until you find the right dilution ratio, as this will depend on the tartness of the juice. It should be well flavoured but not overpowering.
Bring the juice to the boil, and then take the pan off the heat. Stir in the thickened potato starch, and continue to stir until the sauce is clear and shiny with good consistency.
Serve the red juice sauce warm or at room temperature.

INDEX

This English language edition published in 2016 by

Grub Street

4 Rainham Close

London

SW11 6SS

Email: food@grubstreet.co.uk

Twitter: @grub_street

Facebook: Grub Street Publishing

Web: www.grubstreet.co.uk

Text copyright © Marie Holm, 2015

Published originally in Danish under the title *Budding & andre dirrende desserter*

Copyright for the Danish edition © People's Press, 2015

Photographs: Line Thit Klein and Chris Tonnesen

Art direction and styling: Marie Holm

Portrait styling: Tine Berg

Thanks to Mikka Wulff for testing out the recipes.

Thanks to Ditte Ingemann, Line Thit Klein, Tanja Vibe and Julie Bonde Buck / Uh la la Ceramics for lending material for the artwork.

A CIP record for this title is available from the British Library

ISBN 978-1-910690-27-7

Printed and bound in the Czech Republic